# SURVIVAL FOODS

## 70 NUTRIENT-PACKED, EASILY STORED FOODS TO STOCKPILE IN PREPARATION FOR ANY DISASTER

### SEB LARSEN

# CONTENTS

# The Disaster Preparation Item Checklist

**(Essential tools and items for disaster survival)**

## This checklist includes:

- The top 10 most critical items and tools for survival
- Where you can buy each item at an affordable price

**Never get caught unprepared.**

**To receive your checklist, visit the link below:**

https://cedarpathbooks.activehosted.com/f/3

# INTRODUCTION

*"Near the gates and within two cities there will be scourges the like of which was never seen: famine within plague, people put out by steel, crying to the great immortal God for relief."*

— *NOSTRADAMUS*

In a worst-case scenario, what should you stock up on?

Chances are, most people wouldn't know how to correctly answer this question. Some might shout the first thing that comes to mind, like fruits or vegetables, but this would be incorrect, unless you were planning to freeze or preserve them for later. Not knowing the correct answer to this question, and not knowing what foods to stock up on can lead to a compound crisis later on. The time to start thinking about living through a crisis isn't when the crisis occurs: it's before there even is a potential threat.

When a natural disaster or pandemic occurs, most people panic. What food they have in their home is only able to sustain them for a day or two, and when an emergency occurs it could be weeks before they can get to a store. Even when you are able to get to the store to stock up, the shelves offer little for you to choose from and you will have to fight with others for whatever is left.

No one ever thinks it could happen, but few things are certain, and disaster can strike at any moment with most people being completely unprepared. Having even a small stock of food that can get you through a month can be a life saving measure during a time of emergency. If you haven't started preparing, now is the time to do so.

The need for safe, healthy food stores is not just reserved for times of crisis or tragedy. There are entire populations who suffer from hunger across the world. For days, these families face debilitating conditions, missing meals and suffering from malnutrition as a result of a lack of access to proper nutrition.

Consider the recent natural disasters that have compromised entire cities and regions for months. Hurricane Harvey, which devastated the state of Texas in 2017, stranded communities and left them without access to safely preserved food stores for weeks. The recent earthquakes around the world have had an equal if not more devastating effect on communities, suspending access to food and clean water across entire geographic regions. While these disasters are catastrophic to begin with, it is the lack of access to safe and clean food in the wake of these events which impacts long term survivability.

Even in our current times, countries around the world are seeing a surge in grocery sales leaving the shelves bare, with people unsure of when products will be restocked. Very few are taking the current situation seriously, and even the ones who are struggling from its effects are hesitant to stock up on essential items. Some, however, are.

As an urban planner and nutritionist, I have traveled across the world studying various communities and populations. I have had the privilege to help people in these communities gain access to that which many in first world countries take for granted. Through my research, there has always been a significant question which has puzzled me: If we acknowledge that we are not immune to suffering during times of crisis, why are we still so underprepared when these events occur?

There is a good chance that many of the people you know, perhaps even you, wouldn't know how to survive through a state of emergency, without access to food, for an extended period of time. We as a society have distanced ourselves from this fundamental knowledge, and as a result have placed ourselves in a precarious position.

Having an emergency food supply is one the best precautions you can take to give yourself a chance of long term survival after a crisis. Creating an emergency food and water supply gives you the peace of mind that, despite what might happen in the rest of the world, you and your family will be prepared for what is to come.

Over the years, I have helped hundreds of people learn to create sustainable methods of living. From starting community gardens, to building food storage facilities, I have helped people ensure that they and their families have the means to sustain themselves, even when they can't go to the grocery store. In recent times, I have realized how many don't have access to this critical knowledge, and it was the recognition of this fact that inspired me to write this book.

The focus of this book is to outline exactly what one would need at home in order to survive a disaster, or state of emergency when food supply lines are cut. The information and knowledge contained is designed to be easily retained, with step-by-step, easy to follow instructions. After reading this book, you will learn how to not only better prepare for a potential disaster, but how to live a life of long-term, self-sufficient nourishment. Don't put off preparing, it's time to get started now.

# PART I

The first half of this book breaks down the various crisis scenarios that can leave you without access to food or water, and why many people are so ill-prepared for these situations. The purpose of this section is to provide some context for why disaster preparation and food stockpiling is necessary. You will also learn how our natural sensibilities for survival have been suppressed and forgotten over generations, and how these primal understandings can still help us live self-sufficiently today.

After gaining an honest view of the unstable state of the world, you will see the real importance of creating a food strategy for when the inevitable occurs. Knowing what your body needs to survive will give you a clear picture of how you are eating currently, and how a time of crisis can drastically alter you food consumption habits. You will learn the importance of macro and micronutrients, and the importance of stocking these sources of nutrition to create a life-sustaining food supply.

With this information, you will then be shown ways to determine how long the foods you buy will last, their nutritional value, and how you can properly store these foods for optimal longevity. The information up to that point will then guide you to make the best choices in how much and of what to fill your supply with.

If you are looking for a way to better preserve your foods, save money, and build your food supply more quickly, the preservation techniques in the last chapter of this section will contain that information. There, you will acquire some of the most effective methods to store your foods, including traditional techniques that were used by our ancestors, and methods which are commonly used today in homes across the world.

Let your survival planning journey begin!

1

## IN A TIME OF CRISIS...

"Preppers", as they are commonly referred to, are often viewed as overly prepared individuals who obsess over having the right supplies on hand for an apocalyptic situation. While some of these individuals can be quite extreme, many have a realistic idea of what is going on in the world. Preparing for a crisis isn't something one does because they are overdramatizing a situation: they do so because they want to ensure they and their families are safe if disaster strikes.

Natural and man-made disasters can arise without notice. Some disasters can be a combination of both. In any crisis situation, our defaulted survival skills kick in and panic often ensues. Our world is simply not fit to encounter widespread chaos, but it is something that happens throughout history. When we can't rely on our survival skills, we need to rely on the skills we do have with the things we have available. We need to be realist that our world is not in ideal standing, and even the most prosperous countries can suffer from food and water shortages.

## Our World is Fragile

No country or person is immune from confronting disaster that can strike without warning. There are a number of tragedies that can occur that can leave us without the ability to shop and get the essentials that we need to survive. As it has been made clear through history, sudden economical, social, or health crises arise quickly and can keep us in isolation and limited on the foods we have available. Even in today's world we are not exempt from encountering bombings, fires, famine, and pandemics.

The world we live in is unstable. With countries and leaders debating over control of imports, exports, oil, and territories, war is not something that we only hear about from our parents or grandparents: it is something that we may see repeated in our time. In times where military action is needed to protect a country against a threat, supplies for our essentials can run short, or pricing can become too inflamed and most families may not be able to afford the food on the shelves. This has happened throughout history: Europe experienced it during World War II, the United States just before then had suffered through the Great Depression, and the populations of many countries experience widespread poverty. We never think that it can happen to us: this is the exact mindset that leaves so many unprepared.

Aside from conflict that can spark a mass shortage, natural factors also have an impact on one's ability to properly feed themselves and their families. Climate changes around the world are creating problems for farmers, who are struggling to grow sustainable crops to feed people around the world. Long periods of droughts are leaving acres of land dry and depleted. Rising sea levels and rivers are flooding regions and leaving them too waterlogged to plant. Miles of land that would have been ideal for food production has been wiped out.

Storm systems are causing just as much disaster. Earthquakes are causing cities to crumble, tornados are blowing towns to nothing more than debris, hurricanes and tsunamis are engulfing areas. Fires from draughts are destroying everything within their reach. These natural disasters are occurring more frequently, with more severity, and in more areas than ever imagined before. Families are left with nothing, and it can be days or weeks before help comes their way. Natural disasters can leave entire cities and regions devastated. They can cripple a community and completely cut residents off from being able to buy food they need. One can be left with absolutely nothing. Having a stockpile of food set aside that you can easily access ensures that you and your loved ones will be able to eat as you ride out the cleanup and recovery process.

It is a frightening thought to have to worry about a natural disaster occurring. Especially if you are in an area where things like this are uncommon. But, what about events that impact your finances, like losing a job? Unemployment may be the most common circumstance that can leave one unable to buy food and supplies. The job market is completely unstable and everyone is disposable: you never know when a company is going to suddenly go bankrupt, close, or budget cuts need to be made. Many people already know and understand what it's like to be without an income or have their income cut in half. One is often left to make choices between paying the bills or feeding the family. It is not a position one wants to be in, but it is a burden that many may have to face. A serious illness or injury can also cause you to go weeks, months or more without pay. This is a time when one can be even more affected by a loss of income, since it means that the healthier foods that can speed up your recovery may no longer be accessible or affordable.

We may not have control over what happens, but we can be prepared for when the unexpected does happen. To think that such things as war, famine, natural disaster, or pandemics can't occur to you is not only foolish, but dangerous.

## Survival is a Strategy

Knutson, S.

Survival is no longer a natural instinct for us. Our world has grown so accustomed to convenience, grab and go, and oversized proportions, that we rarely think about how we would maintain our health if we didn't have these easy options. Most people aren't eating for the benefits their food can provide them: they reach for food based on their taste and personal preferences.

While our ancestors had natural abilities and understanding of survival, these instincts have weakened over time as things have become easier and accessible for humans. Our ancestors knew they needed to hunt and gather a set amount of food in order to be able to eat for the next few days. They learned how to utilize simple preservation techniques that would allow them to have a supply of food on hand when they knew that food would be scarce.

Even today, those who live in harsh climates seem to be the only individuals who tend to prepare and even know how to create a substantial food storage that can last them for months. Those living in urban and rural settings, where food doesn't have to be hunted, grown, or scavenged, take for granted that they will always have such easy accessibility to food supplies.

We don't think of ever having to fear not being able to drive to the closest grocery store to get what we need or want. This ease of access has, in times of disaster, lead whole communities to panic and be faced with fear about how they will eat for the next few days or even weeks. Until we are in the moment and we actually need to consider what our basic needs are, do we realize how negligent we have been about ensuring we are taking care of our food and provisions needs?

All individuals have just a few basic needs when it comes to survival. Food and water are the most essential, aside from of course the air we breathe. Since we naturally don't allow our survival instincts to kick in, we need to have a survival plan already in place for when we are met with a crisis or unforeseen event that causes us to question whether we could survive or not. We don't want to find ourselves stuck in a situation where we are coming up with solutions as we go.

In times of crisis, everyone tends to default to the same thinking: buy as much as I can as quickly as I can. This causes stores' shelves to quickly become bare and unable to keep up with the demand. What makes this worse is that if deliveries can't be made, the stores remain empty. A few lucky individuals may have enough to get through the first days or maybe even a week, but they will soon find themselves panicking and wondering what to do next. A strategic plan needs to be set way before the crisis hits so we can avoid the panic and fear that takes over people and causes us to buy up what we can without thinking.

Even though we may be granted a bit of time to prepare for a disaster to strike, this often is not enough. We may have alerts of a storm system heading our way, or catch news stories about troubling times in our country, or even read about the warning of a serious health concern that spreads like wildfire. Even after a week's notice, we would barely be able to stock our home with enough food to last for a long period of time. When we know there is a threat coming, everyone runs to the stores and little can be bought. During times of crisis you may be limited in how much you can buy of certain products: for example, you may only be able to get a case of water, or be limited to two canned goods. This is barely enough to make it through a day or two. How can you possibly feed a family for days with so little to go on?

We may not know when exactly an unfortunate event will occur, but we can have some control over our ability to remain calm when it does. The first step is building up an emergency supply of food and water. While you are stocking up, you can take note of the ways you can utilize these foods to ensure that you and your family will have healthy foods to get through a lengthy stay at home or a supermarket food shortage.

**Stocking Up at the Supermarket**

The first thing that comes to mind when creating a food supply strategy is where to purchase these foods. The go-to place will automatically be the local grocery store. This is where people normally buy all their usual products, like fresh foods, bottled water, and a long list of goods that can be considered essential. While supermarkets are the most convenient place to get all the foods you need to create a stockpile, there are many things that need to be kept in mind as one goes.

It is true that foods in the supermarket have long shelf lives because of industrial development. Despite this fact, many manufacturers do not use basic conservation techniques we originally acquired from our ancestors. Instead, foods are stripped of their nutrients, pumped with chemicals, and artificially flavored to taste better than they originally would.

This problem with most store-bought foods containing a number of chemicals, or food that have been genetically modified is that they lack a number of the nutrients that we need to survive. For years, we have brought these items into our homes, fed our families with them, and they are what we turn to in time of need. These foods have hindered our body's natural ability to remain healthy on its own. Relying on these unhealthy foods in a time of crisis is something you want to avoid.

By creating a food strategy, you can ensure that you and your family are stocked up with the right foods. A food strategy will also make the foods you have available last longer. This was the key thinking of our ancestors before we had the convenience of refrigerators and freezers. They needed to make use of what they had available and make it last for days, weeks, or even months at a time. They didn't have fancy machines, man made chemicals, or lab tested ingredients. They only had what they could find in their surroundings. They survived for hundreds of years using simple machines. If they were able to accomplish that without modern advancements, in today's world it should be even easier for us to accomplish.

When we are considering keeping a food reserve, we need to stock enough foods that will last long enough while also meeting our nutritional needs. This requires us to look at only our absolute essentials. Yes, we could have a number of different foods stocked up on, but most likely many of the foods you have in mind will lack the proper nutrients that will keep you healthy and alive for an extended period of time.

This book will cover nutrient-rich foods that can be stored and last a long time. You can buy these foods directly from the local supermarket, or try your hand at different food conservation techniques to have a wider selection and more versatility with your stored foods.

An emergency food storage can relieve you of stress when times of crisis occur. It gives you peace of mind knowing that, even when you can't get to the store or the shelves are bare, you have what you need already to survive times of uncertainty. Understanding what one needs to survive and ensuring your bases are covered will help you start with a small food strategy plan that you can add to and grow. You will discover methods that will preserve your food so you can save money as you prepare for the unexpected. An emergency food supply is something everyone should have in their home, for the long term struggles one may encounter, as well as the short term disasters that can suddenly arise.

You don't want to wait until the money has run out of your bank account, the store shelves are bare, or you are quarantined and unable to leave your home. You want to begin to build your food supply now, so that when the difficult time occurs you won't be stressed or left anxious about how you will manage. Creating the right strategy to be prepared begins by knowing which foods are the best to stock up on. In the next chapter, you will learn exactly what you need to maintain your health during uncertain times and how you should approach creating an emergency food supply today.

# 2

# WHAT YOU NEED TO EAT TO STAY ALIVE

The human body needs a list of complex calories and macronutrients to survive to stay alive. Unfortunately, we have lost sight of the purpose of the foods we eat. Nutritional value is rarely discussed when it comes to planning out meals and very few people understand why we need to eat more of one food group instead of another. This lack of understanding has transformed our world into one that overconsume, overindulge, and deprive our bodies of what they really need while filling them with what causes them to function more slowly, painfully, and improperly.

## Over-Consumption

Society as a whole is one of consumption, and often over-consumption. This is evident in what we buy, what we read, how we relax, and especially in how we eat. Food consumption isn't about providing the body with what it needs. Instead, it is

Zarifi, K.

more about social interaction or convenience. With the ability to stop for coffee, burgers, taco bowls, and sweets from a vending machine, we are never far from being able to just grab something and go. With the rise of online ordering and megastores, people can easily do their grocery shopping through the day without worrying about getting anything aside from what they need for the day.

We have moved away from the traditional sit-down, home-cooked meals to ones that come pre-made and ready to go. This makes it more likely for us to overspend and over consume on the food front. When it comes to the foods we eat, we are more focused on how much time we can save during the meal prepping process. We want to limit the time we spend shopping, cooking, or cleaning up after the meal. Little concern is giving to how substantial the meal is. For most, pre-packaged and pre-cooked meals can cut back the time spent in all these areas.

The problem with pre-packed and cooked meals is there is little nutritional value. Our body is almost never satisfied for long and we feel hungry again quickly because it doesn't get what it needs from those meals. We consume more to feel full, only to repeat the pattern again multiple times in the day. This constant feeling of being hungry makes us think we need to keep consuming more.

We think we simply need more than what we are providing the body. The issue with consuming for convenience isn't just consuming more foods that offer no nutritional value; it also has to do with the portions we eat. We rarely look at how many servings are in these pre-packaged goods. We simply eat until we can't anymore, never realizing that what we were supposed to have is a meal that could last for days, not just one dinner. There is a major shift that has occurred that makes us think we need to increase how much we eat at one meal. This has to do with portion sizes. If you have ever compared the size of the dinner plates or bowls used in most modern homes today to those used in the early 1900s, you will notice that there is a significant size difference. Portions are exuberantly larger and visually seeing these larger portions makes us feel as though we have to consume more, because we have to fill our plates.

We don't need to consume more foods; we need to focus on including more variety in our foods. When creating a stockpile, you want to ensure that every member of the household will have enough to eat for prolonged periods of time. This often averages out to be about half a can to one can of food per person per day. Each family will have a different amount of food they need in order to survive. You have to keep in mind how active everyone is, and their age. Those who are more active will often consume more, younger children may not consume as much. To be better prepared and stock up on the right quantity of food, you will want to track how much each person in your family typically eats in a day. Once you have this better understanding, you can adjust how big your stockpile should be.

**Letting Go of Indulgences**

When creating a food strategy plan, by default we will automatically think of the foods we enjoy eating. Chocolate, cookies, baked goods, and chips will pop up in our attempt to create a stockpile. We don't want to fill our stockpile with this stuff. It can be easy to have plenty of food on hand, but if it isn't providing you with the proper nutrition, it won't do us much good. We want our food supply to last, and we want it to be relatively inexpensive to maintain. This means we need to focus on the bare minimum of food needed to be consumed to stay healthy and fit.

This is problematic for various reasons. One is that we are so accustomed to being able to give in to our cravings at any time, and two, what we tend to indulge in isn't always the healthiest choice for us. Finally, overspending on high-end foods is not always the most viable option when it comes to prepping for a crisis. We may love to treat ourselves with certain foods or meals, but we need to let go of this thinking when we are stockpiling. This isn't to say the foods you stock up on should be boring and bland. An effective stockpile will offer you a variety of meal options that can be flavorful and satisfying.

For the most part, we want to leave out the sweets and foods that aren't meant to last in the long run. We will have to put what we would like to consume every day because it tastes good on the back and take a serious look at only stocking the foods that will help us survive. It is hard to think in this way but, thinking in any other manner is not taking what could occur seriously. It can be funny to say you'll just stock up on candy bars and potato chips, but when you are in a situation where you need more substantial foods, only having these items on hand isn't going to be as fun as it sounds.

**Factors to Consider When Stocking Foods**

When you are beginning to build up your food supply, there are three main factors you want to keep in mind.

**Nutrients**

Nutrients are the chemical compounds our body needs to function and remain healthy. We need a good mix of nutrients such as vitamins, minerals, fats, and carbohydrates to maintain optimal health. When we consider foods to keep stored in case of an emergency, we need to ensure these foods will meet our nutritional needs. They need to have the right balance of micro and macronutrients and have little of the harmful chemicals.

**Durability**

Foods should have a long shelf life. If we are ever in a situation where getting to the grocery store is not a possibility or if anything were to occur that caused the stores to run out of certain items, we need to ensure we have plenty on hand that will get us through until the next shopping trip. Durable goods will retain their nutrition values and freshness for extended periods of time.

**Affordability**

We need our stockpile to be affordable. Think about how much you spend in a week or in a month on groceries. When you consider that you want to have at least two weeks' worth of food on hand, and up to three or more months for a major crisis situation, then you are looking at spending a great deal of money. Building up a supply of foods can take some time, because it can add up to a good amount of money that you might not have right now. But you can start off with just building an emergency food and water supply, which is roughly three days worth of food and water. From there, you can simply spend an extra five dollars each grocery store visit on buying staples to add to your food supply.

**What Does the Body Need in Terms of Nutrients, Vitamins, and Calories for a Healthy Diet?**

The human body relies on a wide range of nutrients, vitamins, and a set number of calories to function properly. It can be easy to neglect these vital components our body needs because most foods only offer a few of the key components. Knowing what we need to stay healthy will help us stock our pantry with the foods that will provide us with what it needs.

It is vital that all the essential nutrients the body needs are obtained over the course of the day. Many of these perform tasks individually on their own, but most of them also work in combination with other nutrients to perform specific functions.

*Proteins*

Protein is necessary for every cell in the body to remain healthy. We build muscles from the protein we eat, and it also keeps our bones strong and skin elastic. Most of our protein comes from animal products like red meats and chicken. These sources of protein provide us with the necessary amino acid to stay healthy. We can also get a wide variety of protein from plant-based sources such as nuts, beans, and grains. If we are sticking to plant-based sources of protein for health or personal reasons, we need to keep in mind that we need to consume a number of different foods in order to receive the total number of amino acids our body needs. Plant protein has an incomplete meaning, there is no single source that meets our protein needs. Our body is also unable to store protein in the same way in which it stores fat and carbohydrates: this means we need to ensure we consume the right proteins every day to stay healthy.

*Carbohydrates*

Carbohydrates are converted into blood sugar which is distributed to the cells, tissues, and muscles in the body as a supply of energy. Excess sugars that have been converted are then stored in the liver and muscles until it is needed. There are two main types of carbohydrates: complex and simple.

Simple carbohydrates are often natural or added sugars. Complex carbohydrates are found in various grains, starchy vegetables (like potatoes), and legumes.

*Fats*

Despite being told that we should limit our consumption of fat, our bodies need certain fats to survive. Essential fatty acids are vital for our body and we are unable to produce it ourselves. We use certain fats as a source of energy.

Saturated fats are common in full-fat dairy products and oils. These fats should be consumed in moderation. Trans fats are another type of dietary fat that can cause a significant rise in blood pressure: these are found in many snack foods. We want to limit our consumption of saturated fats to less than 30 grams a day, and try to eliminate trans fats if possible.

Polyunsaturated fats consist of omega-6 and omega-3 fatty acids. They promote brain health. These are found in seafood items and vegetable oils.

You can easily tell the difference between saturated fats and polyunsaturated fats because polyunsaturated fats will remain in a liquid state at room temperature and saturated fats will be solid.

*Fiber*

Fiber is necessary for our digestive tract to function prop-erly. Without it, we can suffer from constipation. Fiber also keeps our cholesterol levels low and our blood sugar levels balanced. We need to consume at least an ounce of fiber a day.

Dietary fiber is a type of carbohydrate and can be found as either soluble or insoluble fiber. Soluble fibers are ones that are easily digested. They dissolve into a gel that helps move food through the digestive tract. These also play a role in lowering cholesterol levels and keeping blood sugars at a healthy level. Insoluble fibers retain water in the stool. This is what makes it softer and allows it to pass through the digestive tract with ease. The results in less strain placed on the intestines to push food through; insoluble fiber regulates bowel movement.

Fiber is necessary to maintain a healthy body because it keeps our body weight at a healthy range. Because of its role in regulating cholesterol and blood sugar, it reduces the risk of developing diabetes and high blood pressure conditions like hypertension. Those who consume the proper amount of fiber in their diet are at a lower risk of cancers like colon cancer and breast cancer.

*Vitamins*

We get most of our vitamins from fresh fruits and vegetables. Stockpiling fresh produce isn't possible since they spoil quickly, so we will need to consider alternatives to have on hand in the event that we are cut off from purchasing fresh produce due to a crisis. We will go into more details in Chapter 8 on how we can ensure that our body gets the proper vitamins when fresh fruits and vegetables are not an option.

*Minerals*

There are a number of minerals our body needs to stay healthy. These elements are necessary to help the body grow, perform specific functions, and maintain overall health. Minerals are used in a number of ways, from transferring energy in food to our cells, to producing hormones and even regulating the heartbeat. There are a number of minerals our body can benefit from, which will need to be considered when we are choosing foods to stock up on.

*Water*

While our bodies may be able to last a few weeks without food, we can only last a few days without water. The human body consists of nearly 75% percent of water, and we need to maintain this percentage to be healthy. Not only do we need plenty of water just to stay hydrated, but water is also essential for our bodies to be able to absorb the proper vitamins and minerals we need.

Our body expels water a number of ways throughout the day. Sweating, bowel movements, and even breathing, all cause us to lose water. When our body becomes dehydrated, it can throw off our entire system. Even when we are mildly dehydrated, we can suffer from headaches and a lack of energy. Severe cases of dehydration can cause sunken eyes, lower blood pressure, increased heart rate, fevers, and even loss of consciousness.

We rarely consume enough water to stay hydrated during the day. Many people drink sugar-filled drinks, caffeinated beverages, and other liquids that do not properly hydrate the body. In a time of crisis, we need to have enough water to be able to survive, and thankfully, it can be one of the easiest things to stock up on.

Water can be easily stored in a small area of your home. We need to consume about half our body weight in ounces of water a day: this averages out to be about three and a half liters for men and two and a half liters for women. Keep in mind that some of the water you consume can also come from food sources.

Water bought from the stores should be replaced prior to the expiration date listed on the product. If you are filling your own containers to store water, label them with the date they were filled on, and replace them every six months. Ensure that the containers you use are sealed tightly and keep them out of direct sunlight, especially if using plastic containers to store your water in.

## Macro and Micronutrients

The nutrients our body needs can be divided into two specific categories: macronutrients and micronutrients. We need to consume the right balance of each to maintain optimal health.

Macronutrients have specific roles in our bodies. They primarily supply our cells, tissues, muscle, and organs with the right energy and nutrients. Macronutrients are found in every food we consume and consist of fats, proteins, carbohydrates, and we need to consume them in high quantities.

Micronutrients assist macronutrients to help the body function. Micronutrients do not need to be consumed in high quantities, but there are also many more micronutrients that we need on a regular basis. Micronutrients play a role in keeping our energy levels up, regulating our metabolism, monitoring cellular function and they are essential for our overall mental and physical wellbeing. Our macronutrients come from a number of different food sources and there is no one single food that will contain every micronutrient we need. Micronutrients can be divided into three categories:

*Water-soluble vitamins*

These include the B vitamins: thiamine, riboflavin, pyridoxine, and cobalamin. B vitamins are essential for building tissues and developing the nervous systems. Vitamin B1, thiamin, is necessary for us to release energy from the food we consume. Vitamin C, or ascorbic acid, is another essential water-soluble vitamin that is needed to produce growth hormones and keeps our gums, teeth, and bones strong. This vitamin also acts as an antioxidant to keep cells and our immune system healthy. Finally, folic acid is essential for the intestinal tract to function properly, as well as assisting in building DNA and protein.

*Fat-soluble vitamins*

These vitamins include vitamins A, D, E, and K. Vitamin A protects our eyes, skin, and hair. Vitamin D is needed to keep our teeth and bones strong, without it our bones become weak and soft. We need vitamin E to protect our cell membranes to help with blood production. Vitamin K is what helps us heal wounds by aiding in blood clotting.

*Minerals*

We need some specific minerals including calcium, potassium, sodium, iron, and zinc. Calcium is known to help promote strong bones and teeth, but it also aids blood clotting and is needed to keep our nerves and muscles functioning properly. Potassium is what helps regulate our heart rhythm and keep the water in our cells balanced. It is also vital for nerve functions. Sodium helps stimulate the nerves and it also keeps our water levels balanced. Iron is what helps move oxygen through the body and promotes blood cell growth. Zinc plays a role in key functions like moving carbon dioxide through the body, healing wounds, and producing enzymes.

Water is also considered a micronutrient that is necessary to protect the cells, tissues, and organs in our body. It also helps keep the eyes, nose, mouth, and joints lubricated and is needed to maintain the proper body temperature. Water is as essential for us to be able to provide oxygen and nutrients to the cells in our body.

In total there are at least 25 vitamins and minerals the body can benefit from, but only a handful of them are essential for the proper functioning and development of the body. The essential vitamins and minerals you want to ensure you stock up on are covered in greater detail later in this book.

**How to Calculate the Minimum Caloric Intake**

Calories are often given a bad reputation. Just about every diet plan you read about tells you to cut calories from your diet which makes us all believe that they must not be good for us. Calories, however, translate to the energy the food or meal provides your body. If our body isn't being supplied enough energy, we can quickly fall into malnutrition. Even if you do not have an active lifestyle, the body still uses a substantial amount of energy just at rest.

Not consuming the right amount of calories can have serious negative effects on our physical and mental health. When we deprive our bodies of the calories they need, we will often suffer from:

- Depression
- Hysteria
- Hypochondriasis (thinking there is something wrong with our health when there isn't)
- Emotional distress
- Withdraw
- Inability to concentrate
- Impaired judgment
- Low energy

We need calories to keep our body temperature at the

optimal level. More than half of the calories we consume go towards this task alone. If there isn't enough energy in the body, it will begin hunting out internal sources. It will first break down the stored fat in the body, and once it goes through this stored energy source, it will begin to break down our own muscle tissue and even internal organs so they can be converted to energy.

Men typically need around 1500 calories a day and women should aim to consume 12oo a day. This is the bare minimum that will keep your body function properly. These calories will come from a mixture of carbohydrates, proteins, and fats. We can divide our calorie intake according to how much fat, protein, and carbohydrates we need to consume on a daily basis to ensure we are getting the right amount of calories from the proper sources.

Nearly 50% of our calorie intake should come from carbohydrates. If you are a more active individual, you will want to increase your carbohydrates by 10 to 20%. Each gram of carbohydrate we consume will convert to four calories. We can get these carbohydrates from whole grain, dairy, and whole fruits.

Protein should make up about 20% of your calorie intake. Those who are more active will consume a little more protein to fuel the muscles they use regularly. Each gram of protein equals four calories.

Up to 30% of the calories we consume should consist of healthy fats, this is roughly 400 calories from fat for men and around 350 fat calories for women.

You can better understand and calculate your dietary needs by using a number of available nutritional calculators. This can help you set exactly what percent of fats, activity level, body mass and more to show what you need to consume to maintain optimal health. This can be valuable information when you are creating your food storage plan, because it gives you a reference to what you need to include in your food supply. You can also use these calculators to determine what you should be eating with each meal.

# 3

# CHECK YOUR PACKAGES

The first step is knowing what your body needs. The second step is to ensure you are meeting those needs by paying attention to what is on food labels and packaging. Food labels are not always straightforward. There is a great deal of information on these labels that most people never pay attention to or notice. The food label will be one of the first things you look at when you are deciding on what products to buy to grow your food supply. Understanding what the nutritional facts, ingredients, and servings size actually mean will ensure that you are only purchasing products that will provide you with the most benefits.

**Food Labels**

Food labels give you a comprehensive look at what is in the foods you are about to buy and consume. Food labels need to be examined when you are looking for the best foods to stock up on, as the packaging may indicate that the products don't contain certain items but the food label will most likely reveal another story.

### *Servings Sizes*

The first thing that needs to be looked at is the serving size. This is found at the top of the food label and will give you a clear idea of how many servings you should get from that package. Serving size and portion size are not the same. Portion size, as we mentioned early, is the amount you actually eat at the meal. Servings size is the size you can consume provided with the nutritional values indicated on the labels. Servings size can either be shown as just a number or as a unit of measurements like cups or tablespoons.

The serving size is determined by looking at the reference amount customarily consumed (RACC) or the average amount that a person is likely to eat of that item. The RACC is expressed in grams and nutritional values in each RCAA are taken into consideration. Servings size on packages are based off of old data and often reflects much smaller amounts that would be the customarily consumed by today's standards. They still are useful in determining how much one can expect to get out of the products they buy.

### *Nutritional Facts*

The food label also provides you with the nutritional facts. It gives you information on how much of macro and micronutrient is included, as well as the suggested daily value. The daily value percentage (%DV), is the amount of that specific item that you should consume for the day or the percentage you shouldn't exceed in a day. On food labels, this is typically based on a 2000 calorie diet. If the food label states that a nutrient has less than 5% DV, it is considered a low amount, those that have 20% or more DV are considered to be a high source of that nutrient. This is good to keep in mind as you will want to make sure you are choosing the right nutrients for stockpiling.,

The nutritional facts tend to relate to the serving size, or what may be included in the whole package.

### Ingredient Lists

There is also an ingredient list at the bottom of the label, generally after the nutritional facts. The ingredient list can cause a great deal of confusion as the ingredients are listed by their more 'scientific' names as opposed to what most of the general public knows them as. For instance, sugar is often not listed as just sugar, but it is listed as the specific type of sugar used in the food preparation, such as high fructose corn syrup, beet sugar or sorbitol; sugar can also be listed as an artificial sweetener like aspartame, sucralose, and neotame.

What to keep in mind when reviewing the ingredient list is that they are listed by quantity. The ingredients that make up most of the products are listed at the top, and the ingredients that are included in small or trace amounts are listed at the end of the list. This is good to know when you are looking for the healthiest option.

### Check Expiry Dates

Expiration dates will show up on products in a number of ways:

- The sell by date is provided by the manufacturer. This is common on meat, poultry, egg, and dairy products and it lets buyers know when the store should have sold the product by.
- The use by date refers to when the foods will have reached their peak in quality. Using these foods after this date will result in the foods being less flavorful,

or they could even be stale. Foods like bread will often begin to spoil after this date.

- The best if used by date, or use before date, lets you know when the food will have the best quality and flavor. This doesn't mean the foods need to be sold by that date, or that the food will be bad after that date.

These dates are not to ensure consumer safety, or are even required to be displayed on products. Manufacturers place these dates on their products to give consumers a better idea of when foods should be eaten by, in order to reduce the risk of the food becoming moldy or spoiling. It also allows you to know when you can expect the best quality and flavors of that food.

We want to purchase foods to stock up on that have the furthest away expiration dates. The longer the product lasts, the better to stock up on. Some foods can be stored for up to 30 years.

## Optimal Storing Conditions in Your Home

Lostak, M.

Where we plan to keep our stockpile of food can have an impact on the longevity of certain items. The environment can increase the potential for certain foods to spoil faster than usual. Bacteria and mold will flourish in certain environments.

Certain areas of the home can make for ideal conditions for food storage, while others should be completely avoided. When it comes to storing your emergency food supply, there are specific factors that need to be considered and accounted for.

*Humidity levels*

Humidity refers to the amount of water vapor in the air. The temperature in a room can affect humidity levels: as the temperature rises, the amount of moisture that can be held will increase, so the warmer a room is the higher the humidity levels can become. High humidity levels increase the risk of foods becoming exposed to moisture that can cause bacteria and mold to grow.

*Sun exposure*

You will want to keep most of your foods out of direct sunlight. Exposure to sunlight will cause the temperature to rise, and the high heat can destroy your emergency food storage.

*Room temperature*

The temperature of the room should be ideally below 70 degrees F and no more than 80. The lower the temperature in the room, the longer the foods tend to last; the temperature should not fluctuate much either. Basements are an ideal setting for this reason, but pantries can also be a great alternative. A garage can also be used to store foods when there is no basement, but this runs the risk of the temperature becoming too high when the weather is warm.

**Storage Options**

Having a dedicated area or room for your food supply is ideal. A small area in the basement where you can put up some shelves or cabinets to hold your food is a quick solution. You can utilize large storage containers that are partially indestructible to store foods in as well. This can help you stock up on non-perishable items, like boxed pasta, canned foods, or bags of rice, but what about more perishable foods? While it can be incredibly hard to have a wide variety of fresh fruits and vegetables on hand that will last for a long time, you can consider the following options when you want to include fresh produce to your stockpile.

There are additional ways you can store foods to ensure that they remain safe to eat.

### Clay Pot Cooler / Pot-in-Pot

Before there were refrigerators in every house, people needed to use what was available to them to preserve foods. Thousands of years ago, clay pot coolers were used regularly to keep foods cool, and some communities around the world still rely on this method of "refrigeration" to store and keep foods cool. It involves placing a small clay pot inside another large one; the gap between the two pots is filled in with sand, and water is poured on top of the sand. The food is placed in the smaller pot and then covered with a wet cloth. The concept is that the water that is poured into the sand begins to evaporate and draws heat away from the center, where the food is placed.

The pots used must be made of clay or terra cotta, because these pots are porous, which aids in the evaporation process. If you want to give this a try, buy clay pots that are unglazed. It is better to use medium-sized pots (18" or smaller are the best), because smaller containers are easier to keep cool. Aside from the pots, all you need is sand and water, and you have an effective cooling system for your foods.

Some emergency events can leave you without power for long periods of time, which means you won't be able to rely on the refrigerator to keep foods from spoiling. Clay pot cooling is an easy to use method that can be assembled and ready in no time at all. It may not get as cold as a refrigerator, but it can become cool enough to keep a variety of fresh fruits and vegetables from spoiling. When stored in the ideal setting these pots can maintain a temperature of 40 degrees F. The pots are best stored in shaded areas where they are exposed to a breeze which will help keep the pots at a lower temperature.

### Root Cellar

Root cellars used to be commonplace in every home, and are still utilized by civilizations in colder areas of the world. A root cellar uses the natural moisture in the area to preserve foods so that they can be stored for months at a time. A root cellar can be built to store a number of vegetables like potatoes, onions, and carrots, as well as to hold jarred foods.

Root cellars are typically built into the ground to allow the natural elements of the soil to keep the area cold. When building a root cellar, you want to ensure that the area can maintain a cool temperature, around 32 to 40 degrees F, with a humidity level around 90 percent. These cooler, high humidity conditions stop the growth of microorganisms which can promote decomposition.

Root cellar units can be built near your home but can take time and effort, as well as money. You will need to place shelving, have a ventilation system in place, and ensure the cellar has the proper insulation to keep heat out of the area. If you are planning on using your root cellar as a regular form of storage, this can be an ideal option. But if you are in a situation where you need a quick solution, an easier option is to use a hole-in-the-ground method. This can be done quickly, but it does require you to consider proper drainage. For this method to work, you will want to choose a spot that can be dug into the side of a slope. Using a metal garbage can in the hole-in -ground root cellar can keep water from destroying your supply. You'll want your hole to be slightly bigger than the size of garbage you are using to store the food in. The top of the can should come out about four inches from the ground. Then you will need to add straw or dried leaves inside the can, and place durable plastic on top of the straw. Once you have everything in place, you can add your fruit and vegetables, and place the lid on the can, then cover it with a layer of dirt. Your produce will stay cool and fresh.

### Cold Cupboard

Cold pantries or cold cupboards used to be the preferred methods for storing everyday household items like eggs, fruits, and butter. If you are left without power, you may be able to keep items at the appropriate storing temperature with a cold cupboard. This method entails using grates made of metal or wood to bring up the cold air from below your home. There are vents in place at the top of the cupboard which allows for warm air to rise and be pushed out of the area. This allows for the temperature in the cupboard to remain lower than the temperature inside the home.

These cupboards take time to design and build to ensure there is proper ventilation. You will want to include plenty of shelving in your cupboard, so that fruits and vegetables can be laid out in a single layer. These cupboards are also a great place to store any jars or cans of homemade foods you have filled on your own.

### Storing After Opening

Once a product is open, its shelf life decreases significantly. Some food items may only last for a few days, while others can be kept for a few months, and very few foods will still be good after a year. Properly storing open food items increases their longevity, reducing waste.

You want to ensure all dry products such as pasta, rice, grains, and beans are stored in an airtight container so that moisture won't seep in and ruin them. Once these items have been opened, they can be transferred from their original package to plastic containers and placed on the counter for weeks, and they will still be good to use. Most items will still need to be stored away from direct sunlight, so having a cupboard or pantry in or near the kitchen is ideal.

Canned foods and jarred foods will often need to be stored in the refrigerator and used within a few days after opening. You want to transfer stored-bought canned items to an airtight container after opening. Additionally, many of these items can be stored in the freezer for up to three months, which can reduce how much food you are wasting and can help your emergency supply balance.

**Other Considerations**

Another factor to consider when storing your foods is accessibility for insects and rodents. When storing foods, you don't want to just place boxed or plastic bags on the shelf. These can be easily chewed through by mice, and other pests can make their way in even from the tiniest of holes. If possible, you want to store items in glass containers or thick storage bins.

Adding bay leaves to food storage containers is also a natural way to repel insects: placing bay leaves on the shelves or in the corners of your storage unit or pantry will reduce the risk of any bugs contaminating your foods.

Most items can be kept in their original packaging, but you

will want to place boxes or plastic-wrapped items in a heavy-duty plastic container. To ensure that your food hasn't been contaminated by pests, check your items regularly.

Also, keep in mind that you will want to keep your foods in a scheduled rotation. When you rotate your supplies, you can better ensure that your stockpile is filled with foods that aren't going to go bad soon. Cook what has the closest expiration date and restock what you use. Place the newer items in the back of your pantry so you know to use the ones upfront first. Track the foods you have on hand, and organize them by the closest use by date to the furthest away. Keeping track of what you have as you begin to grow your supply will help you see what you need more of, and what you will need to replace soon.

# 4

# TRY AT-HOME CONSERVATION TECHNIQUES

Stocking up on store-bought items may seem like the easiest and most convenient option to build up a sizable food supply, but it can become quite expensive, especially when you also need to consider how much you will need to keep on hand, and if you do not properly research the best deals. Additionally, we need to keep in mind that most of the foods we obtain at supermarkets can do us more harm than good. Packaging, transporting, and exposure to external elements can cause foods from the supermarkets to be tainted, and this results in foods spoiling at a much faster rate than you realize. Many of these factors are unknown to us until we open the packages up to use, and we find ourselves in the situation where we need to throw the food away and move on to plan B. Most of us don't have a plan B.

The way foods are packaged will have an effect on their shelf life. We have covered how one can properly store foods in their home to ensure that elements such as humidity, oxygen, light, and heat won't cause the foods to spoil faster; now we will dive into how you can cut back on your spending by doing some of the canning and jarring yourself. The methods listed in this chapter were once commonly used by everyone to ensure they had enough food on hand to get through long periods of time where buying wouldn't be an option. These methods not only help you save money, but allow you to have complete control over what goes into and what is left out of the foods you keep in your pantry.

Akuptsova

### Why Use At-home Preservation Techniques?

These techniques can help you extend the longevity of your foods. While some foods will last longer if stored in the freezer or refrigerator, the foods listed in this book are meant to be stored in a cool, dry environment. Many of the foods you will buy will be canned or jarred, which you can easily do in your own home. Home preservation techniques also help reduce waste for foods that tend to spoil quickly, like fruits and vegetables, and it allows for you to stock up on the foods that you actually enjoy.

Preserving your own foods isn't something that you can do just to build up an emergency food supply; it is something that you can benefit on a regular basis. Do-it-yourself preservation is a way to increase the sustainability of your food supply all year round. You can increase the longevity of your foods by vacuum sealing or storing items in an air-tight container. There are various ways you can accomplish this.

When using any of the listed techniques, it is advised that you use an easy and organized labeling method. You can do this in a number of ways, but all you need is a permanent marker. Be sure to write the date (month and year) clearly on the packaging, so you know what you need to use first: this will give you a better idea of when you need to use it.

## PRESERVATION TECHNIQUES

### Canning

Canning is an easy way for you to begin building up your emergency food storage. This method has been used for centuries: in the process, you cook foods to a certain temperature, which kills off the bacteria, and seal it as it cools. There are different approaches you can take to canning, and some specific methods need to be used when you plan to can certain foods. The easiest and most popular method of canning is done using warm / hot water baths. This technique doesn't require much: just mason jars, water bath canner, canning kit, lemon juice or citric acid, and thongs. In this process, the jars are placed in a pot of warm water, with the lids on, and they slowly seal themselves. This method is safe to use for a variety of jams, syrups, pickled foods, tomato sauce, and salsas or other acid foods. Items that include tomatoes, such as salsa and sauces need to have a pH level that is below 4.6, so that there isn't a risk of botulism. You may need to experiment with a few different recipes to ensure the pH level is in a safe range.

To use the water canning method, you want to place a large pot of water on your stove. You want to fill the pot with enough water so that the jars will be covered most of the way, while also leaving enough room at the top so that the water can boil around it without splashing into it. Inside the pot you want to place a rack to allow the jars to sit on, so they are not exposed directly to the bottom of the pot. Fill your jars with the ingredient you want and wipe the rims of the jar to remove any spilled over. Screw the lids onto the jars and then place them in your large pot of water. Turn the heat to high and let the water boil. Let the jars sit in the boiling water for ten minutes. As the water boils, you want to place a few kitchen towels on your counter, so you have a spot ready to transfer the jars to cool on once they are done boiling. Turn off the heat and carefully remove the jars from the pot using your canning tongs. Set the jars on the towels and allow them to cool for at least 12 hours. As they cool, they will make a popping sound indicating that the lids have sealed into place.

Pressure canning is another form of canning that uses a pressure system to seal the jars. This method is used for non-acid foods like most vegetables, soups, and meats. You cannot use a traditional canning method for these types of foods because it will not ensure that all bacteria is killed off in the process. You can purchase a pressure canning appliance, which looks fairly similar to traditional pressure cookers. These are fairly affordable and the cost makes up for itself when you see how much food you can stock up and save by owning one. You will need to follow the instructions for the model you purchase.

It is important that you properly sterilize the mason jars and lids and allow them to air dry completely. This needs to be done whether you are using the warm water or pressure cooker method.

When you have your jars cooled and sealed, store them in a dark cool room until you are ready to use them.

Some items you will want to consider canning are tomatoes, peppers, cabbage, apples or applesauce, chicken soup, vegetable soup, stews, blueberries, tomato sauce, green beans, meat chili, and carrots. This is the method you will want to use the most when building an emergency food supply. Since the foods are already fully cooked, they can be served right from the jar. This can be especially valuable when you are in an emergency situation where you don't have power, water, or heat to cook meals.

### Sun drying

Sun drying is a method that has been used by humans since our earliest ancestors, but is best done when the temperature outside is at least 100 degrees F. This is a lengthy process and it can take several days until the food is fully dried, and it can be hindered by changing weather conditions. While the foods are drying, you will want to bring them indoors overnight, so the cooler temperatures do not slow the process down.

Sun-dried fruits or vegetables should be covered with a cheesecloth while they are outdoors so that insects cannot get to them. Once the items have been thoroughly sun-dried, you want to store them in a cool, dark place. The temperature of the room should be under 60 degrees F. Dried foods can be stored in airtight containers, vacuum-sealed bags or in canning jars. When stored properly, they can be kept for four months. Once dried foods have been opened, they are exposed to air and moisture which makes them more susceptible to spoilage, and they should be consumed within a week.

### Smoking

Smoking is primarily done with a variety of meats. A covered grill or meat smoker is all you need to complete this at home preservation technique. If using a grill, you want to be sure to place a pan of water on top of the wood you will burn, and position it just under the meat to reduce the risk of charring the meat.

Keep in mind that most smoked meats will need to be kept in the freezer for a long shelf life, and can also be stored in the refrigerator for up to four days.

### Dried meats

When you make your own dried meats, they can be stored for up to two months. When choosing meats to dry, you want to go with leaner meat that has little fat, as fat will cause the meat to spoil faster, so you also want to be sure to trim your meats before you dry them. Making your own dried meats gives you more control over the process and will help you avoid the preservatives that most store-bought jerky contains.

You can use cured or uncured meats for the drying process You can also buy uncured meats and add a store-bought cure of your own. Using a store-bought cure blend will add flavor to your dried jerky, and will add in some preservatives which can increase its storage length. The longer you allow the meat to dry, the longer its longevity.

You want to use thinly sliced pieces of meat for the drying process. You can also marinate them before you get started. Once they have been removed from the marinade, use a paper towel to remove any excess liquid. You can use a food dehydrator, oven or sun drying method to dry meats. To use a dehydrator, just follow the instructions in the user manual. To use your oven, you will want to set the temperature to 140 degrees F. Place the sliced meat on a baking sheet, ensuring that the strips of meat do not touch or overlap. Place the baking sheet into the oven and allow the meat to cook for four hours: you will want to flip it after about two hours. When ready, the meat should have a firm texture but still be slightly flexible.

When storing dried meat, keep it in an air-tight container with oxygen absorbers and out of the sunlight. Leaving dried mats in sunlight can cause condensation to build up in the packaging which will spoil the meat. If you do notice that there is condensation in the bag you are storing the jerky in, this means you didn't allow it to dry for long enough. You can remove it from the bag and place it back in your oven. To avoid this happening, before packaging your dried meat, allow it to cool completely for at least seven hours. After it has dried completely, place the meat in a brown paper and let it sit for a day or two. This storing step ensures the meat releases any excess moisture, which allows for it to be stored for longer. Use a vacuum sealer to remove as much of the air as possible, and don't forget to add your food-grade oxygen absorber.

### Dehydrating

You can dehydrate both fruits and vegetables: making your own dehydrated fruits and vegetables can significantly increase their shelf life when you store them properly. Dehydrating fruits, vegetables, and other treats help preserve their nutritional value; when stored properly, they can be kept for long periods of time. For dehydrating, you will want to have airtight packaging and oxygen absorbers - mylar bags are the most recommended bags to store dehydrated foods in. It is important that all moisture is removed for the longest shelf life. Oxygen absorbers help ensure that no oxygen builds up in the packaging as it sits. They are added to many packaged foods that you find in the grocery store, but most store-bought packages of dehydrated foods will reabsorb small amounts of moisture while it is being packaged, which results in it spoiling sooner than if done properly at home.

Dehydrated foods, when stored properly can have a shelf life of up to 15 years, and some items can even be stored for longer. Raisins, apricots, and apples have some of the longest shelf lives of up to 30 years. Carrots can usually be stored for up to 20.

You can use a food dehydrator or your oven for this method. To use your oven, preheat it to 225 degrees F. Cut your fruits or vegetables into small bite-sized pieces. For the best results, use fruits and vegetables that are ripe but have maintained a little bit of firmness to them. If you want your fruits to have a little more sweetness to them, sprinkle a little bit of sugar over them. Transfer your cut fruit or vegetables to a baking sheet lined with parchment paper: make sure that they are in a single layer and not overlapping. Place the baking sheet into the oven and allow them to bake for about four hours, checking on them every hour. If you notice that the juices are starting to run out of the fruits, you will want to baste them every hour until they are done. When the edges have become dried and the fruits or vegetables have shriveled, they will be done. Remove them from the oven and transfer them to a cooling rack.

When cooled completely, transfer the fruits or vegetables to an airtight container to vacuum seal them, so they can last longer.

### Jams and jellies

Jams and jellies are a great way to use any fruits that you don't want to see go bad. When choosing fruits to turn into jams, you want to stick with ones that are high in pectins such as apples, plums, and pears. Pectin is also great for easing digestive or stomach issues. If you want to use other fruits for jams, you can buy pectin in liquid or powder form.

When stored in the refrigerator, jams and jellies can stay good for up to three weeks, they can also be stored in the freezer for up to six months. When you have made your own fruit preserve, you can use the warm jarring method to store your homemade jam. An easy to make jam recipe for those who want to give this method a try is strawberry jam. You can use any fruit you like, and the amount of sugar that is added will depend on your taste preference. Taste test as you go to see if you want your jam to be sweeter.

JAM RECIPE

### Ingredients

- 2 pounds of fresh strawberries, stems removed, cut in half.
- 2 cups white sugar (add more if you want an even sweeter jam)
- ½ cup of lemon juice, freshly squeezed is best but you can use store-bought organic juice as well.

### Directions

1. Place your cut strawberries into a large mixing bowl and begin to mash them using a fork or potato masher. Crush the strawberries down until you have four cups of the mashed berries.
2. Place a large saucepan on your stove. You want to use a pan that has a heavy bottom so you don't burn the strawberries in the cooking process. Turn the heat to medium and add in the lemon juice and sugar.

3. Once the sugar has been dissolved in your crushed berries, turn the heat to high. Bring to a boil while stirring frequently. Allow the mixture to boil for ten minutes then turn the heat off and allow the jam to cool down.

To test if the jam is ready to be canned you want to place a spoonful of it on a plate once it has been boiling for ten minutes. Place the plate into your freezer for a minute then remove the plate and draw a line in the jam using your pinky finger or the end of a spoon. The jam will be ready for you to jar when you are able to draw a clear line in it. This ensures that it will form a jelly. If a line doesn't form, you will want to boil the mixture longer.

### Pickling

Pickling is another traditional preservation technique that can be used to prolong the shelf life of your vegetables and fruits. Most pickled foods stored in a glass container and kept out of the sunlight will last for up to a year in your stockpile.

Pickling uses salt, vinegar or alcohol to keep the foods fresh. There are different ways you can approach pickling. You can place the fruits or vegetables into a brine to cure for a few weeks, or you can boil or simmer fresh fruits and vegetables in a brine or spice syrup. Fruit and vegetable relish can also be made from cooked foods.

If you are new to pickling, you can give this easy dill pickle recipe a try.

PICKLING RECIPE

## Ingredients

- 8 pounds of small cucumber, cut into spears
- 30 fresh dill sprigs
- 2 large red onions, sliced thin
- 10 cloves of crushed garlic
- ½ cup of sugar
- ½ cup of salt
- 1 quart of water
- 1 quart of white wine vinegar

## Directions

1. Place the cucumber spear, dill sprigs, sliced onions, and crushed garlic into a large mixing bowl. Toss them together, then set to the side.
2. Place a large pot on the stove and pour in the water, vinegar, salt and sugar. Turn the heat to high and bring everything to a boil. Once the sugar and the salt have completely dissolved, turn the heat off.
3. Pour the water and vinegar mixture into the mixing bowl with the pickles and onions. Allow the mixing bowl to sit on the counter for a few hours to cool.
4. Transfer the mixture to jars for canning while still warm.

You can use the warm water canning process or pressure canning process to preserve the flavors and increase the longevity of your homemade pickles' recipe.

## Salting

Salting is a food preserving technique that was used for

decades prior to refrigerators coming into existence. It is best used for preserving meats and fish. This is a fairly simple process where you coat the foods in thick layers of salt; the salt extracts moisture from the food which reduces the risk of bacterial growth. Once the food has about an inch thick layer of salt coat on it, it needs to be hung to dry, or it can be pickled.

### Fermenting

Fermentation accelerates the decay of food, which is the opposite of what all the other methods listed here do. Most foods that are fermented are transformed into a liquid, such as grapes being fermented into wine, honey used to ferment mead, apples used to ferment cider, and grains used to produce beer. One can also ferment milk to make cheese. Sauerkraut is the most commonly known type of fermented food. To make your own sauerkraut follow the simple steps below.

SAUERKRAUT

### What you will need:

- Mixing bowl
- Cutting board
- Knife
- 2-quart mason jar
- A jelly jar that is small enough to fit into the 2-quart mason jar
- Marbles or clean stones to weigh down the jelly jar
- Cheesecloth
- Rubber band

You will also need a head of cabbage and about 1 ½ teaspoon kosher salt.

**Directions:**

To start, you need to ensure that everything you will be using is properly cleaned. Clean the mason jar, jelly jar, marbles, and stones and allow everything to dry thoroughly. Once everything is cleaned, we can begin!

1. Prepare the cabbage. Remove wilted or flimsy leaves. Trim out the core and then slice the head in half, then in quarters, then cut each quarter lengthwise, and you should have about eight wedges. Take each wedge and thinly slice the leaves so you are left with handfuls of ribbons.
2. Transfer the cabbage ribbons into a large mixing bowl and cover them with the kosher salt. Use your hands to massage the salt into the cabbage. As you massage the cabbage it should become watery and limp. Do this for about ten minutes until your cabbage is tender.
3. Take your 2-quart mason jar and begin adding the salted cabbage to it. Pack the cabbage down until it is all nicely contained in the jar. Any leftover liquids that were in the original bowl with the cabbage should be poured into the mason jar.
4. Put the jelly jar on top of the cabbage to keep it weighed down. Fill the jelly jar with your stones or marbles. Keep in mind this jelly jar will eventually be submerged in liquids during the fermenting process, so you want to ensure that it has a lid which is securely on.
5. Once the jelly has been added to your mason jar, you

want to cover the jar with cheesecloth and keep it in place using a rubber band.

6. Allow the jar to sit in a cool, dark area for 24 hours. During this time you will want to press the cabbage down using the jelly jar every couple of hours. Some liquid should begin to release from the cabbage.

7. After 24 hours the water should have risen over the cabbage. If this does not occur, then you will want to add more liquids to it. Do this by dissolving a teaspoon of salt into a cup of water, then slowly pour the salted water over the cabbage so that it just covers the top of it.

8. Once the cabbage has released enough liquids, you can jar it and allow it to continue to ferment until you are ready to use, or let it sit for three days. After three days, give it a taste test to see if it needs to sit longer. When you are satisfied with the taste, screw the lid on the mason jar and store it in the refrigerator until you are ready to enjoy it.

**Additional Tips**

Freeze-dried foods are also a great option for keeping your food supply fully stocked, but this isn't a method that can be easily done at home. It is best to order freeze-dried food from a knowledgeable seller. You can find a wide array of foods and meals that are easy to store and more lightweight than the cans and bags in typical supply storage units. The biggest benefit of freeze-dried items is that they have the longest shelf life, up to 30 years! Freeze-dried foods are the most cost-efficient way to maintain a food supply stash but they can also be incredibly beneficial to have when there is a situation that results in a food shortage.

Consider a communal exchange with your neighbors -

where you can exchange foods with your neighbors and friends. Throwing a community party is also a great idea when there are foods you need to rotate out of your stockpile, to replace them with fresher ones.

Though using your own preserving techniques will help you stretch your foods for longer, if you are unsure of how long something has been sitting, it is best to throw it out. better be safe than sorry, and avoid having to make a trip to the hospital because you used something that had already spoiled.

# PART II

In the next chapters, you will be introduced to 70 different foods that can be easily found and purchased at your local super-markets. These foods are ideal for crisis situations where there is the potential for food short-ages occurring. The foods included in the list have been picked because they have an acceptable nutritional value and are long-lasting. They are highly affordable and can be even cheaper if you utilize the conservation techniques mentioned in part 1.

Shrewsberry, R.

Remember, this is not about hoarding, it's about buying smart for the long term. You want to be realistic about what you need to have on hand and be aware that having more in the house can lead to overeating. This is why it is important to stock up on the foods that will provide you with the most nutritional value, as opposed to the snack foods that you may be more tempted to eat just because you have them in the pantry.

If you are used to an organic diet, sticking to it might not be the best option for a disaster scenario. Organic foods, though claiming to have more nutritional value than their non-organic counterparts, they are often more expensive and have shorter shelf lives. Additionally, many items that claim to be organic actually aren't organic. This is a common issue, which is why reading the labels before you buy anything is so important.

As you go through the list of foods in the next pages, keep in mind what you will actually eat. There is plenty to choose from: you don't have to stock up on everything and you don't want to stock up on foods that no one in the house will eat. Consider what everyone in your family likes to eat, and keep in mind that if you have kids you will likely struggle with some picky eating and preferences. You can get an idea of what your kids would be willing to eat for prolonged periods of time by asking them what foods they would eat over others. Then you will know what you can include in your stockpile that the kids won't fight you too much on having to eat. Keep in mind that you can always change up the flavors of foods with spices, herbs and condiments.

While you want to ensure that you will have a supply of the foods that will keep everyone healthy, you also need to enjoy them: eating things that you enjoy can help keep everyone in better spirits.

# 5

# 30 CANNED FOODS YOU WON'T REGRET BUYING

This chapter focuses on canned foods to keep in your food supply. Many people shy away from canned foods because they are often considered the least nutritious and appealing of the foods one has available regularly. This isn't the case for all canned foods, in fact, many of them can provide you with the same amount of nutrition as their raw form can. This isn't to say that there are not unhealthy and nutritionally stripped canned foods on the market: you just need to know how to pick the right ones.

Canned goods can have some of the longest shelf life if you know what to look for. When stored in the ideal settings, they can last you up to six years, or at least three. Not only are canned foods ideal for their longevity, but because of their durability. Those who live in areas that are prone to flooding can benefit greatly from having a stockpile of canned foods, as water can't easily seep into sealed cans.

**Shopping for Canned Foods**

Every time you head to the store for your weekly shopping, you can easily grab a can or two of vegetables or meats to add to your food supply. There are a few key guidelines you want to keep in mind and check for as you shop.

PublicDomainArchive

1. When choosing canned foods, you want them to have a low acidic content: these canned goods tend to have a shelf life of up to five years. Higher acidic rate canned foods tend to only have a one to two-year shelf life.

2. Steer away from cans that are dented or damaged, as these are signs that the can has been kept in extreme temperatures.

3. Canned meats are another addition to your stockpile you will want to consider. Canned meats, chicken, tuna, or corn beef have a shelf life of two to five years. When looking at canned meats in the store, be sure to read the labels: you only want meats that have salt and little to no other ingredients listed.

### *A Warning About Store-Bought Canned Foods*

Avoid purchasing canned foods that contain bisphenol - A (BPA) or bisphenol - S (BPS). This is a harmful chemical that is commonly found in the packaging material of canned foods, primarily in the coating of the can. Exposure to these chemicals can cause a number of health issues including an increase of cancer risk, hormonal disruption, and damage to the reproductive system.

### Canned Foods to Consider for Your Stockpile

1. **Canned spinach**: packed with vitamin C, even more than raw spinach, which spoils rather quickly.
2. **Refried beans**: most varieties of refried beans contain high amounts of fiber and protein.
3. **Canned mackerel:** mackerel contains a significant amount of omega-3 fatty acids, B12 vitamins and protein. Mackerel has lower levels of mercury, making it safer to eat than some other fish varieties.
4. **Coconut milk:** great to have on hand as an alternative to dairy options. It offers a wide range of vitamins minerals like Vitamin C and folate.
5. **Canned prunes:** prunes are nutritious, containing a high number of vitamins and minerals. They are an excellent source of vitamin K and C, and they make a great snack. Prunes also have anti-inflammatory properties.
6. **Canned salmon:** canned salmon offers a significant amount of protein and omega-3's. It also provides you with a significant dose of vitamin D and calcium with each serving.
7. **Sardines:** sardines are incredibly good for you and are also highly affordable. These small little fish are packed with omega-3's, vitamin B12, multiple minerals, and calcium. They may be an acquired taste, but they can help keep your nerves functioning properly and your brain healthy. Choose sardines packed in olive oil or water over soybean oil.
8. **Canned corn:** it is great to have a stock of corn kernels on hand as they don't need to be heated to be enjoyed. Add them to salads, soups, or just eat them as a side dish. Corn loses some of its vitamin value during the canning process but maintains its high fiber content.

9. **Canned black olives:** olives contain a high dose of healthy fats which will keep your cholesterol levels in check. They can also give you diet a boost in iron.

10. **Black beans:** high in fiber, antioxidants, protein and a wide range of minerals. Choose canned black beans that have the lowest sodium count and before using or consuming them, drain and rinse them to remove any excess sodium.

11. **Beets:** beets have a special component called betaine which is what gives them their deep color. This promotes heart health and can help reduce the effects of inflammation. Additionally, beets are a great source of fiber, folate, and iron.

12. **Kidney beans:** these beans, like most, are a great source of protein. They are also packed with minerals, vitamins, and fiber. Choose canned kidney beans with no added sugar, sodium, or additives, to receive the most nutritional benefits.

13. **Sauerkraut:** a great probiotic that keeps your gut healthy, also full of vitamins and minerals. The only thing to be cautious about it is that it can come with a high amount of sodium.

14. **Bone broth:** this rich broth is touted for its health benefits as it is nutrient-dense and high in protein. While homemade bone broth will give you the most nutritional value, it is a lengthy process. Canned or jarred bone broth can still provide you with substantial nutrients which you will want in your emergency food stockpile.

15. **Spam:** while it does contain a higher amount of sodium, spam also offers a hefty dose of protein and fat. What is great about having spam in your stockpile is that it can be prepared in a variety of ways, even enjoyed right out of the can.

16. **Chicken:** since it's fully cooked, you don't have to worry about preparing canned chicken. Additionally, canned chicken often has the same nutrients and protein as freshly cooked chicken.

17. **Beef stew:** the combination of potatoes, beef, and carrots means this canned food offers a variety of nutrients. It is packed with protein, iron, and vitamin A.

18. **Artichoke hearts:** an excellent source of vitamins C and K, minerals like magnesium and iron, and are high in fiber.

19. **Canned tuna:** like most fish, tuna is high in omega-3's and also a great source of quality protein. You will also find that tuna provides you with a good amount of vitamin D. When stocking your food supply with tuna, choose canned light tuna.

20. **Pumpkin puree:** packed with essential vitamins that keep the immune system healthy, pumpkin puree also contains six grams of fiber per one cup serving.

21. **Chickpeas:** a great source of plant protein, rich in a number of nutrients. Chickpeas help curb one's appetite, which can be helpful when you have to watch how much you consume to make your food last for a lengthy period of time.

22. **Tomato sauce:** low sodium tomato sauces are a great source of iron and protein. You can choose a meat tomato sauce as well, which will provide you with additional fats and proteins.

23. **Almond butter:** nut butters are great because they can be used as a quick and healthy snack. Almond butter offers six grams of protein and contains 14 grams of healthy fats per serving.

24. **Green beans:** green beans are rich in a number of nutrients like Vitamin K. potassium, magnesium, and

calcium. When canned they can be high in sodium, so it is best to rinse them before you cook them. When cooking, limit the amount of time they cook in water as this can cause them to lose a number of key vitamin sources.

25. **Carrots:** canned carrots are an excellent source of vitamin A. When looking for the right canned carrots, go with a no salt added, or low sodium, option.

26. **Apples:** while not as nutritious as raw apples, canned apples can still provide you with plenty of healthy vitamins like vitamins A, C, and K. Try to avoid getting canned apples that include high fructose corn syrup or other types of added sugars.

27. **Diced tomatoes:** canned diced tomatoes are packed with a number of vitamins and minerals. Be sure to carefully choose canned tomatoes that are packaged in BPA-free materials: the high levels of acidity in tomatoes can cause BPA to leak out into the product more so than with other canned foods.

28. **Yams:** canned yams have a lower sodium level than some of the other canned foods on this list and they are a great source of fiber and various vitamins like vitamins A and C.

29. **Chicken noodle soup**: it is nice to have a few comfort items in your stockpile of food, and chicken noodle soup is one to the most common comfort foods around. This soup is a go-to for many when feeling under the weather. Chicken soup can be a great source of protein, some have up to 10g per serving, and vitamin A. Choose a low-sodium variety that contains less than 300 mg of sodium in each serving to benefit even more from this convenient meal.

30. **Vegetable medley:** this canned option comes with carrots, corn, green beans, peas and often other veggies. It is a great addition to your food supply because you get the benefits from a number of different veggies as opposed to just one.

# 6

## 20 GRAINS AND LEGUMES TO GIVE YOUR BODY FIBER AND PROTEINS

L egumes and grain are your go-to foods. These are the foundations for stockpiling. Pasta, rice, legumes and beans will make up a majority of your stockpile. These foods are essential because they can provide you with sufficient energy and a decent amount of protein.

This chapter will give you some smart shopping tips that will help you when buying grains and legumes, as well as 20 different grains and legumes to explore. You will also find some quick and useful recipes to try out that will allow you to use these items in a variety of recipes.

**Buy in Bulk**

Buying in bulk is ideal when you are building up a food supply for an emergency situation. When you consider that for an average adult you will want to have at least 25 pounds of various grains and at least five pounds of dried beans on hand, this can result in a lot of space being taken up by individual boxes and bags. When you add in the amount of food you will need to feed everyone in your household, it is just not sensible to have 50 or more different boxes of one pound pasta in your basement, or 10 or more small bags of beans piling up. Bulk buying can help you save on both storage space and money.

Bulk buying is an easy way to get more of what you need for less. But when shopping in stores, we can be deceived into thinking that we are buying more than we actually are. Many manufacturers purposefully package products in bigger sized packages: this is done to make us think we are getting more than what we actually are. A larger package does not always equate to more food, and this can cause one to spend more while getting less for their money's worth.

When shopping, it is good to hunt for additional discounts for buying in bulk. Some stores may offer a certain percentage off items when they are bought in bulk as opposed to bought indi-vidually. You can buy boxes or crates of foods that have come

Foodism360

right off the delivery truck with a nice discount. Do a little bit of research beforehand to find the best deals as well. Compare prices and see where you can possibly get a deal on buying two or three of the same products for the price of one. Use coupons or discount codes offered on store websites or through apps for even more savings. Doing a little bit of planning before you shop can save you a substan-tial amount of money.

When you buy in bulk, you make building up your stockpile

more affordable. If you live in an area where there are bulk-buying aisles, take advantage of them. Bulk food aisles allow you to bring your own container to fill with a number of different dried products. You can often find different pastas, rice, oats, beans: by filling your own bins, you can save yourself a significant amount of money.

If the stores near you do not offer this, you can still find a way to get the most out of your money.

### Long-Term Food Suppliers

Long-term food suppliers are those that offer bulk buying options for those who want to stockpile their emergency food supply at an affordable price. You can find a variety of products from these sellers, from dehydrated and freeze-dried meals to bulk packaging of wheat and beans. Buying grains and legumes from a long-term food storage seller will ensure that you get products that have the longest shelf life, as they used special packaging to increase the longevity of these items.

It can be a good idea to get others interested in preparing a food supply to order with you. Some places have a minimum amount that you need to order, which can be easily met if more than just your household is trying to stock up. Ask family and friends if they want to order in bulk and the minimum can be easily met.

### Wholesalers

Many stores or warehouse club stores offer a variety of foods that you can buy in bulk. This will allow you to get enough of what you need all at once. Many of these big stores require you to pay a monthly membership to take advantage of the bulk-buying deals but even with the membership fee, you can often build a stockpile for half the money than you would spend if you were to go through a traditional grocery store.

### Online Shopping

Shopping from an online bulk seller can be another way to save when building your food supply. Many sites offer a nice variety of foods that can be purchased in high quantities and can save you a good amount of money. You'll want to compare prices with your local stores still. While you may be thinking you are getting a great deal, it might only be saving you a few dollars and not all sites offer free shipping, so your savings could average out to be the same.

### Essential Grains and Legumes

Soft grain can be stored for up to eight years depending on their packaging, and hard grains can last for up to 12 years when stored correctly. Hard grains need oxygen absorbers in order for them to have maximum shelf life. Rolled oats are another grain that can offer plenty of servings and can last from two years and up to 30 years. If oats are kept in the store-bought container, they will stay fresh when stored at room temperature. To increase their longevity, you can separate the oats into an airtight container with oxygen absorbers.

Grains and legumes are essential for an emergency food supply because they will be a main source of fibers, proteins, vitamins and more. When shopping for grain and legumes you want to keep in mind the following.

- Whole grains, as opposed to white grains, will provide you with a number of minerals and antioxidants. White, wild, basmati, and jasmine rice can be stored for up to 20 years in the right conditions. Brown rice doesn't last as long but is a healthier option.

- Ground flour does not keep as well as whole grains, which can be stored for up to 25 years in place in an airtight bag and with added oxygen absorbers.
- Dried pasta of all varieties can have a shelf life up to 30 years if it's not exposed to oxygen or moisture in the air. Most store-bought pastas have a shelf life of 2 years past their best by date.
- Dried corn, or popcorn, when kept from moisture can have a shelf life of 15 years or longer.
- Dried beans, legumes, and lentils can be kept for up to five years, but after about three years they tend to take longer to cook and can become so hard that even boiling them won't soften them up.

### *How to Use Them*

Grains and legumes can be used in a number of ways for any meal of the day. Flours can be used to make breads, pancakes, and muffins that can last for a few days. Oats can be used for breakfast and in baked goods.

Rice and quinoa can be used to make healthy breakfasts, lunches, or dinners. These can also be cooked in big batches at the beginning of the week and incorporated into other meals throughout the week.

Beans, legumes, and pastas are great in soups, as side dishes, or as main courses. Beans can be used in place of different meat products in meals. When you are stuck in a lockdown situation where you can't leave you home, this is the best time to experiment with different ways to use these items.

You can get creative with how you use these items. The only drawback from some of these items is they do require presoaking or longer cook times, which may not seem like an ideal option when you want to prepare something quick and healthy. You can avoid having to spend all the extra time cooking by making these items in bigger batches and using them in multiple meals throughout the week. They also freeze well so you can double recipes and use one half for a weeknight dinner and store the other in the freezer to reheat at a later time.

**Grains to Stock Up On**

1. **Barley:** raises good cholesterol levels and also has a variety of essential vitamins and minerals our body needs.
2. **Whole oats:** oats are full of fiber, antioxidants, and nutrients. Eating oats regularly can help lower bad cholesterol levels and maintain blood sugar levels.
3. **Quinoa:** packed with vitamins and nutrients but also a great source of protein. Unlike many other plant-based protein sources, quinoa provides you with all nine of the essential amino acids the body needs to stay healthy. Quinoa can be found as black, red, or white. Each type has more or less, the same nutritional components but can have different taste and textures. You can also find fully cooked ready to serve quinoa that has a two-year shelf life and the added benefit of not having to worry about how to cook it.
4. **Farro:** this grain has one of the higher fiber levels out of the grains listed here; it is also a sufficient source of protein. Farro can be easily stored whole and ground as needed.
5. **Brown rice:** highly nutritious and it contains a number of vitamins and minerals. Like many other

grains, it is also high in fiber and contains antioxidants that will help keep your immune system healthy

6. **Wheat:** whole wheat flour is great to have on hand and as a part of your stockpile. It can be a decent source of fiber, protein, and other minerals. Be sure to choose whole wheat and not refined wheat, which has significantly less nutritional values.

7. **White rice:** highly affordable, which is why it can be a smart addition to your food supply, though in terms of nutritional value it doesn't measure up to some of the other higher priced grains. White rice tends to be enriched with the nutrients that are stripped from it during the process phase. So it will still provide iron, folic acid, and a few other vitamins.

8. **Wholegrain cereals and crackers:** these tend to include different layers of grain like wheat, oats, rye, barley, and millet. These cereals are beneficial because they are high in fiber. When adding wholegrain cereals to your emergency food stock, look for low-sugar cereals that provide at least three grams of fiber per serving. Also go with whole grain cereals that have less than 210mg of sodium in a serving. You will also want to have a few items that can be snacked on, and wholegrain crackers are an ideal option. Many wholegrain crackers are packed with fiber, protein, and B vitamins.

9. **Pasta:** you can find a variety of pasta to stock up, from your standard white pasta, whole wheat pasta, to lentil pasta and black bean pasta. Have a variety in your stockpile that contains the lowest amount of sodium and offers at least five grams of fiber per serving.

10. **Rice flour:** a good source of protein and fiber. This

can be used in a number of recipes and it works incredibly well as a thickening agent for soups and stews.

11. **Granola:** loaded with protein, fiber, iron, B vitamins, vitamin E and more. This is great to eat as a healthy snack, or it can be used to top yogurt or oats. While loose granola is the best option, it can be wise to also stock up on healthy granola bars: kids tend to enjoy those and they are an effortless breakfast or snack option. Just make sure to read the label and choose granola bars with natural ingredients and do not include high fructose corn syrup.

**Legumes to Stock Up On**

A variety of beans will ensure that you have enough protein on hand to survive. They also keep the cholesterol levels in check and can provide anti-inflammatory benefits. While most legumes and beans will be high in fiber, there are additional vitamins and minerals they can provide.

Dried beans are ideal for keeping in your stockpile because of their longevity: they are also fairly easy to cook and add flavor to.

1. **Split peas:** these legumes are high in iron and zinc. They can help combat the effect of hypertension and reduce the risk of prediabetes
2. **Peanuts:** dry peanuts are part of the legume family. Peanuts contain a high level of vitamins and various B vitamins. What makes them a must-have in your stockpile is that they provide you with a significant source of healthy fats.
3. **Garbanzo beans:** better known as chickpeas, they are a significant source of protein and can often be used

as a replacement for meat in many dishes. Chickpeas are also packed with folate, phosphorus, and iron.

4. **Lentils:** lentils can be brown, red, yellow, green, or a specialty variety. Lentils as a whole are packed with protein and essential vitamins and minerals. Green lentils, however, tend to be slightly healthier.

5. **Black-eyed peas:** these are a great source of fiber and iron. What makes black-eyed peas a must-have in your pantry is they are easy to use. They often don't require soaking prior to cooking, like the other beans on this list.

6. **Black beans:** they provide us with a high number of carbs that are primarily composed of soluble fiber. They are also a great source of protein.

7. **Pinto beans:** like most other beans, pinto beans have a high concentration of antioxidants, which can reduce the risk of a number of chronic diseases. They are also a great source of protein and fiber.

8. **Kidney beans:** great to use for soups and chilis as they tend to withstand the higher temperature and longer cooking times better than some other beans. They can provide you with close to eight grams of protein and over six grams of fiber per serving.

9. **Cannellini beans:** they tend to have a creamy texture making them highly versatile. They can provide you with 11 grams of protein per serving as well as a variety of other nutrients.

**Recipes to Try**

You can substitute many of the ingredients in these recipes with the ones you prefer. They all utilize a number of the beans and grains listed previously. Recipes that include only beans and vegetables can be canned at home and added to your food stockpile.

## OVERNIGHT OATS

Most overnight oats are made with milk or a milk substitute like almond or soy milk. This recipe utilizes water so that you preserve the milk if needed; it uses a number of ingredients you should already have in your pantry, but they can all be easily substituted for the flavors you prefer. Additionally, if you can add in fresh fruits, this is a great way to use them up. This recipe makes two servings but can be easily doubled to serve everyone in your family. If you don't want to store the overnight oats in the refrigerator, simply mix everything together in the morning then heat in your microwave or on the stove for a few minutes.

### *Ingredients*

- ½ cup of rolled oats
- 2 tablespoons of cocoa powder
- 4 tablespoon of dried coconut flakes
- 2 tablespoon honey
- ½ cups water
- 2 tablespoons chia seeds

### *Directions*

1. Take a small mixing bowl and add the rolled oats, cocoa powder, dried coconut flakes, and chia seeds. Stir everything together.
2. Pour in the honey and water. Stir, then cover the bowl and place it in the refrigerator.

3. The next morning take out and serve. The mixture can be warmed if you desire.

Overnight oats, when stored in an airtight container, can be kept in the refrigerator for up to five days. The longer they sit, the softer the oats will become.

## PINTO BEANS AND RICE

This recipe also works well with black beans, and can serve as a base for burrito bowls, soups, and even simply salsa. You can serve it as a main course, or use it as a dip for tortilla chips. It is filled with complex carbs, proteins, fiber, and essential vitamins that you will need when surviving a crisis. You can also add canned chicken or cooked ground beef to it to create a different meal each time you make it. This recipe makes about eight servings, so you can have an easy dish that can be served differently a few days throughout the week.

### *Ingredients*

*For the beans:*

- 1 pound of dried pinto beans, sorted to remove any defective beans.
- 1 onion, chopped finely
- ½ tablespoon garlic powder
- ½ teaspoon sea salt
- ½ teaspoon ground black pepper

*For the rice:*

- 2 tablespoon olive oil
- 2 cups white rice
- 1 cup tomato sauce

- 4 cups chicken broth

### Directions

*For the beans:*

1. Soak the beans in a bowl of water overnight or for 24 hours, ensuring that the water covers the beans entirely. You may need to drain and add more as the water is absorbed by the beans. Drain and rinse the beans thoroughly, then transfer the beans to a large pot.
2. Place the pot on your stove and add the chopped onions and garlic powder.
3. Pour enough water into the pot so that the beans are covered and the water rises about two inches above the beans.
4. Turn the heat on high and bring the water to a boil, then reduce the heat to medium-low, cover the pot and allow the beans to simmer for about three hours.

*For the rice:*

1. Place a large skillet on the stove and turn the heat to medium. Add in the olive oil to warm up, then add in the rice. Cook the rice in the oil for a few minutes, stirring frequently.
2. When the rice has turned to a nice golden brown color, pour in the tomato sauce and chicken broth. Turn the heat up to bring to a boil. Stir occasionally.
3. Once the liquids have come to a boil, turn the heat down to low and cover the skillet with a lid. Allow the rice to cook for 15 minutes. Most of the liquid should have been absorbed. Remove the lid and use a

fork to fluff up the rice. Allow it to cook, uncovered, for another five minutes until more liquid evaporates.

Once the rice and the beans have been cooked, you can combine them in a large mixing bowl to mix together. Serve with your favorite toppings, for example shredded cheddar cheese, tomatoes, sliced avocados, or green onions.

## SPIRAL PASTA

This simple pasta dish can be made quickly and with almost any vegetable or meat you want or have available. While you can use fresh vegetables and freshly cooked chicken, if you don't have them available, you can stick with this recipe by incorporating canned vegetables and chicken. This recipe makes for a great dinner, and leftovers can be used for lunch during the week. It makes about six servings.

### *Ingredients*

- 16 ounces packaged of spiral pasta
- 1 can of chicken
- 1 can of spinach
- 1 can of diced tomatoes
- 1 can of crushed tomatoes
- 1 teaspoon oregano
- 1 teaspoon basil
- ½ teaspoon ground black pepper
- ½ cup Parmesan cheese (optional)

### *Directions*

1. Begin by cooking the pasta as directed on the

package.

2. As the pasta cooks, place a large skillet on your stove and turn the heat to medium. Add the canned chicken, diced tomatoes, crushed tomatoes, oregano, basil, and ground black pepper to the skillet. Allow the liquids to come to a boil, then reduce heat to medium-low, and cover. Let everything simmer together for about 10 minutes.

3. Once the pasta is done cooking, drain it, then add it to the large skillet with the other ingredients. Mix everything together and allow to cook for another five minutes. Sprinkle with parmesan cheese if desired. Serve and enjoy.

## QUINOA SALAD

This is a light and refreshing recipe that is packed with vitamins and nutrients. You can add a can of tuna or salmon for a boost of omega-3's and to change it up a bit. While it does require oranges, if you can't buy them fresh, if you have a can of oranges in your stockpile, it can easily be substituted. This makes for a great dinner, side dish, or lunch option.

### Ingredients

- 1 cup of quinoa
- 2 oranges, peeled, divided and cut in half
- 1 cup of black beans
- 1 can of corn (drained)

### For the dressing

- ¼ cup of extra virgin olive oil
- ¼ cup of apple cider vinegar

- ¼ cup of orange juice
- Zest of 1 orange
- ½ tablespoon of sugar

*Directions*

1. Soak the black beans overnight or for 24 hours in a large bowl of water. Drain and rinse the beans once they are done soaking.
2. Place a saucepan on the stove with the 3 cups of water in it. Turn the heat to high and add in your soaked black beans. Bring to a boil, then reduce heat to low, cover, and allow the beans to cook for 2 hours. After two hours, turn the heat off and allow the beans to cool, with the cover still on, for about an hour.
3. Once the beans have cooled, you can begin working with the rest of the ingredients.
4. Place the quinoa in a bowl of water and allow it to soak for 20 minutes. After 20 minutes, drain and rinse the quinoa.
5. Place a large skillet on the stove with two cups of water in it. Transfer the cooked quinoa to the pot of water, bring the water to a boil, then reduce the heat, cover and allow the quinoa to simmer for 20 minutes.
6. As the quinoa cooks, start on the dressing. In a small mixing bowl, combine the extra virgin olive oil, apple cider vinegar, the orange juice, and the zest. Whisk everything together, then cover and place in the refrigerator until ready to use.
7. Once the quinoa is done cooking, transfer it to a large mixing bowl. Add the orange pieces, drained canned corn, and black beans. Mix everything

together, then take the dressing out of the
refrigerator and pour it over the top. Toss so that
everything is nicely coated and serve.

## CHICKEN SOUP

This is a great recipe to make and can. It uses what you have
on hand and you can make plenty of swaps to change it up.
This calls for rice, but you can also use a small pasta or egg
noodle instead. You can even add in corn and black beans
with some taco seasoning like cumin and chili powder to
create a completely different, flavorful soup.

### Ingredients

- 1 can of carrots
- 1 can of corn
- 1 can of chicken
- 1 cup of white rice
- 8 cups of chicken broth
- 1 teaspoon parsley
- 1 teaspoon basil
- ¼ teaspoon sea salt
- ¼ teaspoon ground black pepper

### Directions

1. Place a large soup pot on the stove, turn the heat to
   high. Add the carrots, corn, broth, chicken, white
   rice, parsley, basil, sea salt, and black pepper, stir
   together and bring everything to a boil.
2. Reduce the heat to medium, cover and allow the soup
   to simmer for 30 minutes. Then simply serve and
   enjoy!

# 7 TYPES OF OILS AND VINEGARS TO STOCK UP ON

Oil is the most common ingredient in almost all recipes, this is because it is highly versatile and is primarily used when cooking foods. Vinegars are less used but can assist in preservation techniques and can add flavor to meals. Both items are used in a number of dressings, sauces, marinades, and dips, which can give your meals a flavorful boost. Additionally, they both have long shelf lives and can help keep you healthy.

## Why Stock Up on Oils?

Oils are an essential source of healthy fats and vitamins. Each oil will have a variation of how much fats and which nutrients are present, but they are all beneficial for maintaining good health.

Photosofyou.

Oils are used in cooking foods, but not all oils should be used to do so. Each oil has a different smoke point, which means that at a certain temperature the oil begins to lose its nutritional value. This is why some oils are better reserved for making dressing with, and others are better for frying with.

It is important to understand which oils are healthy for you and which ones can actually cause health problems. All oils have fat, but non-processed oils or unrefined oil have healthier unsaturated fats, making them highly beneficial. Oils that are refined or processed tend to have a significant amount of trans fat, which can cause a number of health problems. Some of the oils that you will want to steer away from when adding to your food supply are avocado oil, soybean oil, shortening, margarine, cottonseed oil, and canola oil. Avocado oil, though healthy, has a short shelf life of only six months. The other oils are unhealthy, mostly are refined or genetically modified and have been hydrogenated, which means that they contain a significant amount of trans fat.

### Why Stock Up on Vinegars?

Vinegars have a distinct sour taste, which is why they aren't always favored in meals. But vinegars have antimicrobial and antioxidant properties. For centuries, various types of vinegar have been used for their medicinal properties.

Vinegar can help keep blood sugar levels and cholesterol levels low. The antimicrobial properties of some vinegars can help treat a number of ailments and better protect the body from infections. Vinegar can also help repair cell damage in the body. Finally, it can be used as a probiotic, promoting the growth of healthy gut bacteria.

Those who have diabetes or prediabetes should seriously consider having a few bottles of vinegar in their food storage. When vinegar is taken just before a meal, it can help keep the glucose, insulin, and triglyceride levels lowered for up to five hours after a meal. Since refilling medications, often needed for diabetics, is not something one may be able to do in times of crisis, knowing how to manage symptoms like increased blood pressure, glucose levels, and insulin levels can literally be a lifesaver. This isn't to say that you should replace your medications with vinegar, but it is something to keep in mind when you have no other options.

Not all vinegars are the same, but they each offer their own unique set of benefits. They can also be infused with a variety of different herbs or fruits to give it a more pleasing flavor.

## Oils and Vinegars to Add to Your Food Supply

When it comes to choosing the right oils and vinegars consider the ones listed here first.

1. **Coconut oil:** extra virgin unrefined coconut oil can be kept unopened in your pantry for up to five years. Once opened, coconut oil can be used for months until you notice it smells bad or yellow spots appear on the rim of the jar lid, it is good to use. It has less cholesterol than other cooking oils and butters. This oil can be especially good for one's health because it does not contain trans fat

2. **Olive oil:** most olive oil will last for two years unopened. To ensure maximum shelf life, store olive oil in a glass, air-tight jar, in a dark place. Extra virgin organic olive oil is best used to make your own dressing and dips, while organic virgin olive oil or organic olive oil is best used for cooking. Olive oil can also be found in a convenient spray form, with the same shelf life of other olive oils.

3. **Corn oil:** organic, non-GMO corn oil contains a high amount of vitamin E and plenty of healthy unsaturated fats. This oil is great to use as a back up oil since it is fairly cheap and has a shelf life of one year.

4. **Ghee:** pure organic, grass-fed ghee offers a number of healthy nutrients when used. This clarified butter has an impressive shelf life when stored properly. Unopened, it can be kept for nine months, once opened it can be used for up to three months if stored at room temperature or for up to a year if kept in the refrigerator. Ghee is actually butter that has had all its water removed. What you are left with is a creamy, high-smoke point, flavorful spread that is ideal for cooking. It is high in omega-3's and vitamins A, D, and K. It has a rich flavor and it tastes a bit like caramelized milk.

5. **White vinegar:** white vinegar can be stored unopened indefinitely. It contains a key component that can fight off pathogens and bacteria in the body. It can fight off infections and improve cardiovascular health while also reducing one's risk of cancer and diabetes. White vinegar also has natural disinfecting properties making it ideal to use in do-it-yourself cleaning supplies. If anyone comes down with the hiccups, having a little sip of white vinegar is said to make them go away.

6. **Apple cider vinegar:** organic apple cider vinegar offers a number of nutrients that can keep you healthy, and it can also be used as an effective natural cleaning product, so you can get a lot of uses out of it both in and out of the kitchen. This vinegar has been traditionally used as a natural remedy for sore throats and digestive issues since it contains

probiotic components. Apple cider vinegar contains special polyphenol chemicals that help heal damaged cells in the body.

7. **Balsamic vinegar:** balsamic vinegar is great for salad dressings, dips, and marinades. It is packed with a number of antioxidants that help keep the body functioning and healthy. When unopened, balsamic vinegar can be stored for up to three years.

## Recap

You have been provided with a lot of information thus far. To make things easier to find and to refer back to, you can use the list below to help with your food strategy. This list breaks down all the foods listed in the previous chapters by category, so it is easier to glance at as a refresher for what you should consider for your food storage.

### Grains

- Quinoa
- Wheat
- Rice flour
- Barley
- Quinoa
- Brown rice
- White rice
- Oats
- Farro
- Wholegrain cereals and crackers
- Pastas

### Legumes (Dried)

- Split Peas

- Peanuts
- Garbanzo beans
- Lentils
- Black-eyes peas
- Black beans
- Pinto beans
- Kidney beans
- Cannellini beans

## Canned Beans

- Refried beans
- Canned black beans
- Canned kidney beans
- Canned chickpeas

## Canned Fruits and Vegetables

- Canned spinach
- Canned prunes
- Canned corn
- Canned black olives
- Canned beets
- Canned sauerkraut
- Canned artichoke hearts
- Canned pumpkin puree
- Canned diced tomatoes
- Canned green beans
- Canned carrots
- Canned apples
- Canned yams
- Canned vegetable medley

## Canned Meats, Poultry and Seafood

- Canned mackerel
- Canned salmon
- Sardines
- Spam
- Canned chicken
- Canned tuna

## Canned Meals and Others

- Coconut milk
- Bone broth
- Beef stew
- Canned tomato sauce
- Almond butter
- Chicken noodle soup

## Healthy Oils

- Coconut oil
- Olive oil
- Corn oil
- Ghee

## Vinegars

- White wine vinegar
- Apple cider vinegar
- Balsamic vinegar

# 8

# 13 VITAMIN, MINERALS, AND SUPPLEMENTS ESSENTIAL FOR YOUR HEALTH

Most essential vitamins are found in fresh or plant-based foods like vegetables and fruits. These items don't have a long shelf life. Root vegetables tend to last longer, so you can stock up on various types of potatoes, garlic, and onions. When you store them in a brown paper bag in a cool and dark place, they can be good to use for a few weeks. Citrus fruits such as lemons, limes, and oranges have the best longevity in terms of fruit, though many others can also be stored in the freezer and used later or added to recipes and then canned and sorted.

When you lack the proper essential vitamins, your body will not function as it should. It is important to keep in mind that during times of crisis where food supplies are limited, supplements might be necessary.

**Supplements to Stock Up on**

If it isn't possible to get your vitamins from natural sources, supplements may be necessary which can be found in supermarkets or pharmacies. While the body can benefit from a long list of vitamins and minerals, there are essential vitamins that are an absolute necessity for the body to properly function and grow. The supplements you will

Gorecki, J.

want to keep on hand will depend on the foods you stock up on. While many vitamins and minerals can be easily consumed through whole grains and legumes that you have stocked up on, vitamin A and C for example may not abound in your stockpiled food and may not be sufficient in these items.

- **Vitamin A:** we need vitamin A to maintain healthy bones, teeth, and skin. It can be found in a variety of darker colored fruits and vegetables. Egg yolk, fish, and beef also contain vitamin A. To ensure proper health, men should ingest around 900mcg/day and women should aim to consume 700mcg/day. Keeping in mind that one can take up to 3000 mcg a day of vitamin A, you want to be careful not to supplement this vitamin too much. When the body gets an excess of vitamin A, it can build up in the body and this can be toxic.
- **B Vitamins:** B vitamins are essential for complete health. There are eight types of B vitamins, also known as vitamin B complex:
- *Vitamin B1 - Thiamine:* B1 vitamins are found in lean meats, nuts, whole grains, and legumes, but the best source to get thiamine from is organ meats. This vitamin is necessary for our body to be able to properly convert the carbohydrates we consume into energy and it's also needed to maintain heart health.

- *Vitamin B2 - Riboflavin:* riboflavin is necessary for the body to produce red blood cells and assist other B vitamins in functioning properly. B2 vitamins can be found naturally in milk, green vegetables, and whole grains.
- *Vitamin B3 - Niacin:* Vitamin B3 helps lower cholesterol levels and is needed to keep the nerves and skin cells of the body healthy. Niacin can be found in high quantities in avocados, eggs, fish. whole grains, and poultry. Men need 16mg of vitamin B3 a day and women need around 14 mg every day.
- *Vitamin B5 - Pantothenic Acid:* we need B5 vitamins to help break down foods and keep cholesterol levels in a healthy range. This B vitamin also plays a role in hormone production. Pantothenic acid can be consumed through avocado, kale, legumes, poultry, and organ meat.
- *Vitamin B6 - Pyridoxine:* vitamin B6 has a number of functions in the body. It keeps the brain healthy, assists with protein synthesis, and is needed for red cell production. Avocado, lean meats, poultry, nuts, legumes, and whole grains can provide the body with vitamin B6. We can consume up to 100 mg of vitamin B6 a day but both men and women only need a little over 1 mg/day.
- *Vitamin B7 - Biotin:* biotin is needed to break down carbohydrates and proteins and is also needed to produce certain hormones in the body. B7 vitamins can be found in egg yolks, legumes, and yeast.
- *Vitamin B12:* B12 vitamins are necessary to maintain metabolism and increase red blood cell production. It also plays a significant role in lower homocysteine levels which can cause damage in the body. The best

foods to get vitamin B12 from include eggs, milk, and seafood.

- **Vitamin C:** vitamin C is an antioxidant that keeps our entire immune system healthy. We need plenty of vitamin C to keep our teeth and gums healthy and to help heal wounds. The best sources to get vitamin C from are a range of fresh fruits and vegetables such as citrus fruits, berries, spinach, cabbage, and broccoli. Since these natural sources are not easy to stock up on in their raw form, taking a supplement can ensure you are getting the right dose of vitamin C regularly. Men need about 90 mg of vitamin C a day and women only need 75 mg a day, although it is safe to consume up to 2000 mg a day to give the immune system more of a boost when it is needed.

- **Vitamin D:** most individuals are deficient in vitamin D, which is primarily absorbed through sun exposure. It can also be found in a variety of fish and fortified cereals. Because many people have a tendency to struggle with getting enough of this vitamin and because it is necessary to help the body properly absorb calcium, a supplement is wise to consider even outside of including it in your stockpile. Those under the age of 70 should be ingesting at least 15 mcg a day of vitamin D or around 600 IUs. Those over 70 need more vitamin D and should aim to get about 20mcg a day or around 800 IUs a day.

- **Vitamin E:** vitamin E is needed to help the production of red blood cells and allows the body to properly absorb and use vitamin K properly. Vitamin E can be found in leafy green vegetables, seeds, nuts, and wheat. We should aim to take about 15mg a day of vitamin E a day, and can take up to 1000 mgs. It is important not to go over the maximum limit with vitamin E because, like vitamin A, it can build up and become toxic to the body.

- **Vitamin K:** we need vitamin K to help blood clot to heal wounds and to maintain proper bone health. Vitamin K is primarily found in eggs, fish, and leafy green vegetables. Vitamin K can also become toxic if one over consumes it in a day.

- **Calcium:** it is already known that we need calcium to keep our bones and teeth healthy and strong. It is also vital for our bodies to be able to form blood clots to heal wounds and for muscles to contract, as well as playing a vital role in monitoring our heartbeat. The most common sources to get calcium from are dairy products which, during times of crisis, may not be readily available. We need about 1000 mg of calcium a day, and as our body doesn't produce it, a supplement is good to have on hand when we cannot get calcium from natural sources.

- **Chromium:** we need chromium to regulate our glucose levels. This mineral is primarily responsible for ensuring that all the cells in the body are supplied with enough energy to function properly. It is found in abundance in fresh vegetables and in a variety of herbs. We need between 25 to 35 mcg a day to keep our insulin levels in check.

- **Folate:** folate works with vitamin B12 in red blood cell production. This is an essential vitamin for women who are pregnant as it is needed to produce DNA. Different beans, citrus fruits, wheat, and leafy green vegetables can supply us with some of our daily folate needs. While we can consume folate from natural sources without limitation, in supplement form is it recommended to take about 400 mcg/day.

- **Iodine:** this mineral plays a vital role in proper thyroid functioning. It helps control hormone release to balance metabolism, aids in body temperature regulation, helps maintain healthy bones, and assists brain development. The recommended daily intake should be around 150 mcg for both men and women and not exceed 1,100 mcg a day.

- **Iron:** iron is a component in most cells in our body, especially the red blood cells. The red blood cells are responsible for transferring oxygen from the lungs to the rest of the body. Without sufficient iron, these cells can't carry enough oxygen to all the organs or tissues. Iron also converts the nutrients we consume into energy. When we don't get enough iron, we suffer from being extremely fatigued, weak, frequent chest pains, difficulty breathing, dizziness, constantly feeling cold, inflammation, and much more. To keep our cells healthy and ensure we are supplying enough oxygen throughout the body, we should aim to supplement no more than 45 mg/day. Ideally, women should aim for 18 mg/ day and men should take about 8mg/day.

- **Magnesium:** our bodies are unable to produce magnesium on their own, but it is one of the most abundant minerals for the human body. This mineral is responsible for keeping the body energized, building proteins, and it also assists in many brain functions that can help regulate our moods. This supplement should be added to an emergency food supply since getting the adequate amounts to ensure our body function properly will be more difficult when we are facing times of high stress and uncertainty. Men and women should supplement their magnesium to ensure they are getting 300 to 350 mg/day.

- **Zinc:** Zinc keeps the immune system working properly and keeps it strong so that it can fight off any bacteria or viral infections. This mineral also impacts our taste and smell senses. Women only need around 8mg a day, while men need about 10mg. Pregnant women will need more zinc to ensure their baby is growing healthy and strong. The best natural source to obtain zinc is from animal meats; though it can also be consumed through plant-based sources, because of the way it breaks down in the body, you'll need to consume twice as much plant-based zinc. This might not be a realistic option when you need to conserve what you eat in a crisis.

**How Long Do Supplements Last?**

Not all supplements will have a sell by or use by date displayed on them. As a general rule, most will have a shelf life of two years, but this depends on the type of supplement: chewables or gummy vitamins have a much shorter shelf life because of their ability to absorb moisture, while tablet or capsule types of vitamins, when stored properly, can last for months or years. Unlike foods, supplements won't pose you harm if consumed past their expiration dates, but they will lose the potency the longer they are stored for.

Vitamins can be kept in their original packaging. If unopened, they should be stored in a cool and dry place for maximum shelf life. Once opened, you want to keep them stored in a temperature-controlled room. Many people keep their vitamin in their bathrooms or kitchen, which exposes them to higher heat and humidity. A bedroom closet or drawer is a much better place to keep your supplements. Some supplements like vitamin E should be stored in the refrigerator if you want to maximize their longevity.

# 9

# 11 SEASONINGS TO MAKE FOOD LESS BLAND

You have all the information you need to start creating your own emergency food supply. However...

While you have the right foods, you need some other things that will help give you more options and keep your meals interesting. When you enjoy the taste of your foods more, you will automatically be put in a better mood. And staying joyful when you are dealing with traumatic times is almost as important as ensuring you are getting the right vitamins and minerals. Stocking up on spices and herbs isn't strictly essential, but they are usually fairly cheap, take up little space, and both dried herbs and spices have decent shelf lives.

## Making Your Own Herbs and Spices

Herbs are created from the leaves of a plant, and can be dried and stored for up to two years, while spices are made from the roots, seeds or bark of

Couleur

the plant and they can be kept for up to four years if they remain unopened and placed in a cool, dark environment. It is incredibly easy to start your own herb garden, and it can be done using a small planter that you can keep on your kitchen counter. Growing your own herbs allows you to have fresh herbs whenever you need or want them.

Fresh herbs are also sold at the local supermarkets and are typically inexpensive. Whether you grow your own or you buy your own herbs, prepping them so you can have a supply in your food supply is a simple process. A bundle of herbs can be tied together around the stems and hung upside down in a paper bag to air dry, or you can use your oven to speed up the process. Using the air-dry method can take up to a week to complete, while using the oven method can have your herbs ready in just a few hours.

To oven-dry, you want to spread your herbs across a baking sheet in a single layer. Turn the oven to no higher than 180 degrees F. Place the baking sheet in the oven and leave the door to the oven open. Check the herbs after two hours to see if they are dry enough. You can check the dryness by testing how easily one of the leaves crumbles. If they crumble with no effort, remove the baking sheet from the oven. If the leaves do not crumble with ease, allow them to continue to bake. Once the leaves are fully dried, you can place them in an airtight container if you plan to use them immediately, or you can use a canning method to seal them so they stay fresh for months.

You don't want to crumble or crush the herbs if you are storing them for a while. It is best to do this just before you add them to meals. Herbs not only give your dishes more flavor, but they can also come packed with a number of beneficial components that can boost your health.

**Herbs and Spices to Stock Up on**

While you have an unlimited number of herbs and spices you can add to your food strategy, there are a few that can provide you with more health benefits. The herbs and spices list here add delicious flavors and give your overall health a powerful boost.

1. **Garlic powder:** garlic powder is made when a bulb of garlic is dried and then ground into a fine powder. Just as raw garlic provides us with a number of health benefits, garlic powder can do the same. Garlic has a little bit of almost every vital nutrient the body needs including vitamin C, B6, fiber, and iron. Because of all the nutrients, it gives your immune system a boost making you less suitable to viruses and infections.

2. **Whole pepper flakes:** often sold in stores as red pepper flakes, this spice is a combination of different dried peppers seeds. Once the seeds have been dried, they are pounded to thin them out. This definitely adds a kick to any dish, but bringing on the heat isn't the only reason you should keep these in your supply stash. Red pepper flakes can boost metabolism, curb hunger, alleviate pain caused by inflammation, and can help protect against certain types of cancers.

3. **Ground cinnamon:** ground cinnamon comes from cinnamon sticks, which you can usually find in the spice section at the supermarket. The sticks are ground and then a fine powder is gathered. Even though cinnamon is considered a sweet spice, it can be added to a number of savory dishes like chili as well. Aside from its pleasant taste, cinnamon has a number of medicinal properties. It provides you with

plenty of antioxidants and has anti-inflammatory properties. Adding just a teaspoon of cinnamon to your meals each day can significantly improve your health and help keep you healthy.

4. **Nutmeg:** nutmeg is ground out of nutmeg seeds that grow from a dark-leaved evergreen tree. Nutmeg can help detox the body and increase functionality of the immune system. Nutmeg can also assist cognitive functions strongly. It has a distinctive taste that offers a bit of sweetness, spice, and nutty flavors.

5. **Cayenne:** cayenne pepper can help alleviate pain, reduce blood pressure, aid in digestion, and increase your metabolism. This spice is made from cayenne peppers which are dried and then ground into a fine powder. This process can include the seeds of the pepper or not. Cayenne has a slightly spicy taste that goes well in almost any dish. Most versions bought in the store include other varieties of peppers and not just cayenne.

6. **Cumin:** cumin is a popular spice in many Spanish dishes. This spice is beneficial because it improves digestion, has a significant amount of iron in it, and can help reduce the risk of one catching a food-borne illness, among many other benefits.

7. **Turmeric:** turmeric is considered a superfood spice. It comes from the dried root of the turmeric plant, and can help keep the whole body healthy and functioning properly. Turmeric has an abundant amount of antioxidants and anti-inflammatories. This spice can also have a positive effect on your mood.

8. **Parsley:** parsley is often overlooked as a useless garnish just added to a plate to give it a little color, but it is actually a powerhouse of vital nutrients. It is

also rich in antioxidants and has special components that support the bone, can help fight off cancer, and can protect the eyes.

9. **Oregano:** a versatile herb that can be used in just about any dish. This common herb has some impressive health benefits: including this herb in your supply stock can help you fight off harmful bacteria and viruses. Oregano can also help reduce inflammation and it contains a number of antioxidants that can support a healthy body.

10. **Basil:** Basil isn't just used to add flavor to dishes, you can add it to tea as well. Basil provides the body with a number of vitamins and minerals as well as antioxidants. It can also improve digestion, skin, and gut health. It has a unique detoxifying component that can help remove free radicals from the body to keep you in good health.

11. **Cloves:** cloves have a very distinct sweet and spicy taste. They can be used to add flavor to meats, beans, and rice dishes. Aside from the flavor boost, cloves have a list of health benefits they can provide you: they can kill bacteria in the body, are high in antioxidants, can help regulate blood sugar levels, and help keep the bones healthy and strong.

## Recap

It can be hard to keep track of all the essentials your food needs to cover when you are stockpiling. Creating a simple checklist can help you locate what nutrients you need to need to get more of.

This checklist breaks down all the foods listed in this book according to the nutrient needs they fulfill. You can use this list as an example of how to create your own or use it to cross off what you already have and what you still need to get.

**Proteins**

- Quinoa
- Canned chicken
- Wheat
- Rice flour
- Refried beans
- Canned mackerel
- Canned tuna
- Canned salmon
- Black beans
- Kidney beans
- Spam
- Chicken
- Beef stew
- Chicken noodle soup
- Vegetable medley
- Chickpeas
- Almond butter
- Garbanzo bean
- Black beans
- Kidney beans
- Pinto beans

**Carbs**

- Barley
- Quinoa
- Brown rice
- White rite
- Oats

- Farro
- Wholegrain cereals and crackers
- Pastas
- Beef stew

## Fats

- Peanuts
- Canned black olives
- Almond butter
- Coconut oil
- Olive oil
- Corn oil
- Ghee

## Fibers

- Oats
- Farro
- Brown rice
- Wholegrain cereals and crackers
- Rice flour
- Granola
- Beets
- Refried beans
- Black beans
- Pumpkin puree
- Yams
- Cannellini beans
- Kidney beans
- Pinto beans
- Black beans
- Black-eyed peas
- Lentils

- Garbanzo beans
- Split peas

## Vitamins and Minerals

- Barley
- Quinoa
- Brown rice
- White rice
- Granola
- Lentils
- Split peas
- Canned spinach
- Canned mackerel
- Canned apples
- Yams
- Coconut milk
- Canned prunes
- Diced tomatoes
- Green beans
- Tomato sauce
- Canned salmon
- Sardines
- Canned corn
- Carrots
- Beets
- Sauerkraut
- Bone broth
- Artichoke hearts
- Pumpkin puree
- White vinegar
- Apple cider vinegar
- Balsamic vinegar
- Supplements

# AFTERWORD

Having a supply of long-lasting foods will be invaluable when you find yourself in the middle of a crisis situation. Though we may be provided with a few days warning before disaster actually strikes, that is never the right time to begin prepping. Imagine what you would have to accomplish in those few days if you found out you had one last chance to go to the store before having to hunker down for a few days or even weeks. A few days may only grant you the ability to stock up with a few days' worth of vital foods, and more than likely, you'll be stuck with whatever is actually left over on the shelves.

We may have not had to live through multiple wars and such severe economic events that left us completely without food, although in some areas around the world this is a reality. But many of us know firsthand the devastation that comes when a natural disaster hits, when one loses a job or becomes seriously ill and unable to work, or even when health pandemics cause countries to shut down. Who knows how long you will have to hunker down at home to leave it only when it is absolutely necessary, and when you do leave, you risk your health and the health of your family. You would feel more secure and safe staying in your home as much as possible.

When you have a food strategy, you can eliminate the need and worry of having to do the food shopping in critical times. Building up a food supply doesn't have to be a long and expensive task. You can start by ensuring you have just three days' worth of food and water for each person in your home. From this three-day emergency supply, you can build a week-long stock, then a month-long one, and eventually, you will find yourself feeling proud and worry-free with your year's worth of food supply.

It is not unlikely that this is something we could all greatly benefit from having. When you take the time to properly plan on what to stock up on, you not only eliminate the stress and worry, but you ensure that you aren't just eating the same boring foods every single day.

This book has outlined the simple steps one can take to build a sustainable, nutritious, and versatile food supply in case of an emergency. You have learned which foods you should ensure to have in abundance and which ones to have a minimum of. Aside from now understanding how to shop for the best food, you also know how you can create canned, dehydrated, and fermented foods yourself, so that you can save money and build your food stockpile even faster.

The recommended foods listed in the second half of the book provide you with a starting point for what you can begin to buy and store so that your most basic nutritional needs are met. You can return to this list as a reference to ensure you have the right amount of food for each person in your home.

When a disaster strikes, the last thing you want to have to worry about on top of all the other unanswerable questions is how well you are going to eat. How will your family eat? How long before you can get to the store? Will there even be anything left to choose from? You can avoid all the worry and fear that comes in these times by creating your own emergency survival food supply. It doesn't take much to get started and starting with a few things is better than not starting at all. Don't wait until you can add a lot to your food supply, add just one thing each time you go to the store and you'd be amazed by how quickly it begins to add up.

It is my hope that by reading through *Survival Foods* you have found a great deal of value; I hope that the knowledge you gained here encourages you to share what you have learned with your friends and family, and share where you found the information. From here, you can go on to learn even more life-sustaining skills like starting your own garden, or filtering your own drinking water from the rain. In a time of crisis, these valuable skills can not only benefit you and your family, but can provide relief to others in need. Please, do not hesitate to leave a positive review if you have found this information helpful.

# REFERENCES

Beans and Rice. (2020, April 6). https://goodcheapeats.-com/beans-and-rice/

Christensen, E. (2020, January 29). How To Make Home-made Sauerkraut in a Mason Jar. https://www.thekitchn.-com/how-to-make-homemade-sauerkraut-in-a-mason-jar-193124

Colino, S. (2017, January 18). The Health Benefits of Vinegar. https://health.usnews.com/wellness/food/articles/2017-01-18/the-health-benefits-of-vinegar

Definitions of Health Terms: Nutrition. (2019, May 8). https://medlineplus.gov/definitions/nutritiondefini-tions.html

DeMunno, L. (2018, July 14). 9 natural disasters that took the lives of hundreds of thousands. https://www.businessinsid-er.com/worst-natural-disasters-2018-7#1975-typhoon-nina-126000-deaths-9

Forni, K. (2018, January 1). Sausage Spinach Pasta Bake.

https://www.tasteofhome.com/recipes/sausage-spinach-pasta-bake/

Frazier, K. (n.d.). Pickle Recipes. https://cooking.lovetoknow.com/pickle-recipes

How to Preserve Your Garden Herbs. (n.d.). https://www.hgtv.com/outdoors/flowers-and-plants/herbs/how-to-preserve-your-garden-herbs

Katharine, Sarah, Richardson, B., & K, P. (2007, September 25). Strawberry Jam Recipe. https://www.allrecipes.com/recipe/38410/strawberry-jam/

Landsverk, G. (2020, March 3). What 3 nutritionists recommend stockpiling for healthy, flavorful meals during a coronavirus quarantine. https://www.businessinsider.com/nutritionists-how-to-prepare-healthy-food-for-quarantine-2020-3

MaxLiving Health Expert MaxLiving, Expert, M. L. H., & MaxLiving. (2019, March 1). Essential Nutrients 101: Your Guide to Nutrition, What You Need, and the Science of Why. https://maxliving.com/healthy-articles/essential-nutrients-101-your-guide-nutrition-what-you-need-and-the-science-of-why

Mega List of 33 Types of Spices Every Kitchen Needs (Photos & Charts). (2019, November 22). https://www.homestratosphere.com/list-of-spices/

Old Farmer's Almanac. (n.d.). Root Cellars: Types and Storage Tips. https://www.almanac.com/content/root-cellars-types-and-storage-tips

Ratini, M. (2018, June 19). Vitamins and Minerals: How Much Should You Take? https://www.webmd.com/vitamins-and-supplements/vitamins-minerals-how-much-should-you-take#3

Rhee, C. (2016, November 4). Black Bean Quinoa Salad. https://damndelicious.net/2014/05/28/black-bean-quinoa-salad/

Russo, J. (n.d.). Emergency Food Storage Explained: Where to Begin and What to Store for Survival. https://geardisciple.com/emergency-food-storage-explained-for-survival/#items-that-will-ruin-your-survival-food

Snell, M. (2019, August 19). Medieval Food Preservation Methods. https://www.thoughtco.com/medieval-food-preservation-1788842

The 13 Vitamins Essential for Survival: NutriFusion Plant-Based Vitamins. (2018, December 26). https://nutrifusion.com/13-vitamins-essential-survival/

Vitamins and Minerals. (n.d.). https://www.nia.nih.gov/health/vitamins-and-minerals

Washington State University. (n.d.). https://mynutrition.wsu.edu/nutrition-basics

## PHOTOGRAPHY CREDIT

Akuptsova. (Photographer). 2016, October. Pickles {digital image}. https://pixabay.com/photos/pickles-billet-cucumbers-1799731/

Couleur (Photographer). 2018, January. Pepper {digital image}. https://pixabay.com/photos/pepper-peppercorns-spices-sharp-3061211/

Foodism360. (Photographer). 2020, May. Whole foods {digital image}. https://unsplash.com/photos/c8WqAPUDsIQ

Gorecki, J. (Photographer). 2019, May. Vitamins {digital image}. https://pixabay.com/photos/vitamins-antibiotics-parsley-diet-4179315/

Knuton, S. (Photographer). 2018, May. Seattle hunger {digital image}. https://unsplash.com/photos/lQ2BzDNmnHE

Lostak, M. (Photographer). 2018, May. Food storage {digital image}. https://unsplash.com/photos/Gzu-sNr19TU

Photosofyou. (Photographer). 2017, October. Oils {digital image}. https://pixabay.com/photos/oil-sale-delicious-healthy-vinegar-2817843/

PublicDomainArchive. (Photographer) 2014, December. Canned foods {digital image} https://pixabay.com/photos/canned-food-cans-supermarket-food-570114/

Shrewsberry, R. (Photographer). 2019, February. Root cellar {digital image}. https://pixabay.com/photos/root-cellar-canned-goods-settlers-4022024/

Zarifi, K. (Photographer). 2019, May. Oversized burger {digital image}. https://unsplash.com/photos/pcST1a65ekI